BIBLE STUDY COMMENTARY

Proverbs–Isaiah 39

Bible Study Commentary

Proverbs–Isaiah 39

CHRIS WRIGHT

Scripture Union
130, City Road, London EC1V 2NJ

CHRISTIAN LITERATURE CRUSADE
Fort Washington, Pennsylvania 19034

© 1983 Scripture Union
130 City Road, London EC1V 2NJ

First published 1983

ISBN 0 86201 115 9 (UK)
ISBN 0 87508 158 4 (USA)

All rights reserved. No part of this publication may be reproduced stored in a retrieval system, or transmitted, in any form or by any means, electronic, mechanical, photocopying, recording or otherwise, without the prior permission of Scripture Union

Phototypeset in Great Britain by
Input Typesetting Ltd., London SW19 8DR.

Printed in Great Britain by
Ebenezer Baylis & Son Limited
The Trinity Press, Worcester, and London.

General Introduction

The worldwide church in the last quarter of the twentieth century faces a number of challenges. In some places the church is growing rapidly and the pressing need is for an adequately trained leadership. Some Christians face persecution and need support and encouragement, while others struggle with the inroads of apathy and secularism. We must come to terms, too, with the challenges presented by Marxism, Humanism, a belief that 'science' can conquer all the ills of mankind, and a whole range of Eastern religions and modern sects. If we are to make anything of this confused and confusing world it demands a faith which is solidly biblical.

Individual Christians, too, in their personal lives face a whole range of different needs – emotional, physical, psychological, mental. As we think more and more about our relationships with one another in the body of Christ and as we explore our various ministries in that body, as we discover new dimensions in worship and as we work at what it means to embody Christ in a fallen world, we need a solid base. And that base can only come through a relationship with Jesus Christ which is firmly founded on biblical truth.

The Bible, however, is not a magical book. It is not enough to say, 'I believe', and quote a few texts selected at random. We must be prepared to work with the text until our whole outlook is moulded by it. We must be ready to question our existing position and ask the true meaning of the word for us in our situation. All this demands careful study not only of the text but also of its background and of our culture. Above all it demands prayerful and expectant looking to the Spirit of God to bring the word creatively to our own hearts and lives.

This new series of books has been commissioned in response to the repeated requests for something new to follow on from Bible Characters and Doctrines. It is now over ten years since the first series of Bible Study Books were produced and it is hoped the new books will reflect the changes of the last ten years and bring the Bible text to life for a new generation of readers. The series has three aims:

1. To encourage regular, systematic, personal Bible reading. Each volume is divided into sections ideally suited to daily use, and will normally provide material for three months (the exceptions being Psalms and 1 Corinthians-Galatians, four months, and Mark and Ezra-Job, two months). Used in this way the books will cover the entire Bible in five years. The comments aim to give background information and enlarge on the meaning of the text, with special reference to the contemporary relevance. Detailed questions of application are, however, often left to the reader. The questions for further study are designed to aid in this respect.

2. To provide a resource manual for group study. These books do not provide a detailed plan for week by week study. Nor do they present a group leader with a complete set of ready-made questions or activity ideas. They do, however, provide the basic biblical material and, in the questions for further discussion, they give starting points for group discussion.

3. To build into a complete Bible commentary. There is, of course, no shortage of commentaries. Here, however, we have a difference. Rather than look at the text verse by verse the writers examine larger blocks of text, preserving the natural flow of the original thought and observing natural breaks.

Writers have based their comments on the Revised Standard Version and some have also used the New International Version in some detail. The books can, however, be used with any version.

Proverbs: Introduction

Proverbs is one of three books in the Old Testament (the others being Job and Ecclesiastes) which make up the 'Wisdom Literature'. These books are, however, only a small deposit of what was a large and vigorous movement within Israel from an early period – the school of 'wise men' (and women – 2 Sam. 14; 20:16–22). Alongside priests and prophets they were a major source of teaching and revelation (Jer. 18:18). Though there was a wisdom tradition before Solomon, he provided an immense stimulus, both by his own work as author and collector, and by the international scope of his empire. He fostered cultural as well as commercial exchanges (1 Kings 4:29–34; 10:1–13, 24). In neighbouring countries, particularly Egypt and Arabia, there was already an ancient wisdom tradition, mostly connected with training for civil or imperial service.

The main concern of Proverbs is to show how wisdom, which is founded on fear of the LORD, applies to the 'small change' of life (personal characteristics that you can't legislate about) just as much as to major state policies or cosmic order. The methods include paternal advice and warning, contrast and simile, observation and prescription, irony and humour. Jesus himself clearly absorbed the contents of Proverbs and perfected its methods in his own teaching.

It is possible to study Proverbs thematically, taking different subjects and tracing them through copious references. But that runs against the grain of the nature of the book itself and its chosen method. Nevertheless, the book does proclaim its own theme motto as '*the fear of the LORD* is the beginning (first principle) of wisdom', and although a cursory reading might give the impression that the book is wholly absorbed with *man*, it is interesting to see how much of the character, behaviour and attitudes that are commended do reflect the character of *God* as revealed elsewhere in the Old Testament. The following examples of this are worth looking for as you read your way through.

1. God is sovereign. Although man has the freedom and responsibility of deliberation and choice, it is God's will that counts in the end. The essence of wisdom, therefore, is to accept this and seek God's guidance. Conversely, the essence of folly is to struggle against it in reckless self-will. The 'fool' in Proverbs is no mere simpleton. In his various guises, especially that of 'scoffer', he is the person whose life is lived deliberately, even boastingly, without reference to God. Wisdom and folly are thus not primarily intellectual, but moral and spiritual, concepts.

2. 'God created man in his own image . . . male and female he created them' (Genesis 1:27). Human sexuality is part of the image of God in man and therefore infinitely precious. The Bible everywhere seeks to protect it from abuse and Proverbs is no exception, with its condemnation of adultery and seduction and its delight in the joys of faithful marriage.

3. God is our Father, and the human parent-child relationship is modelled on that between God and his children. So we find that a lot of the teaching in Proverbs is cast in a 'father-son' form, emphasising authority and humility respectively. We find parental discipline and punishment affirmed as a function, not a denial, of love and we feel the joy or the pain that the child's obedience or stubbornness can cause the parent.

4. God is righteous, both as ruler and as judge. And so we find much in Proverbs about the demands of justice both in the exercise of political authority ('the king') and in judicial activity. Social righteousness is as much a concern of Israel's Wisdom literature as it is of the law and the prophets.

5. God is love. His grace, faithfulness and kindness were 'legendary' in the praises of Israel. So what then is expected of human friendship? The virtues of consideration, tact, kindness, loyalty, forgiveness and generosity are all portrayed in Proverbs.

6. God is compassionate. Israel's national history began with their deliverance from oppression and slavery, and they were commanded to imitate his compassion and practical care for the poor (Deuteronomy 10:17–19, 15:7–11). The same concern motivates many proverbs. The sages, like the prophets, detested the economic injustice that caused and perpetuated poverty. Many of their sayings about wealth and its abuses have a thoroughly modern ring and relevance.

7. God is a worker, whose infinite skill and patience, revealed in his creation (see ch. 8), he has transmitted in finite degree to man, made in his own image. Man too is meant to work. The 'sluggard', therefore, is not just a figure of tragi-comedy; his voluntary and habitual laziness is a denial of his humanity and an insult to his Creator. The enforced idleness of involuntary unemployment is hardly anything less.

8. God speaks. One of the highest gifts of God is man's limitless ability to communicate in language. In this too he reflects his communicating, revealing, speaking Creator. Words matter then, for they, no less than deeds, are powerful vehicles of good and evil. And so we find a lot in Proverbs about our use and abuse of words in a kaleidoscope of situations.

Because all of these concerns are closely related to the unchanging character of God, they have a perennial relevance which transcends the world of ancient Israel. Sometimes this is of burning relevance to the great issues of today's world, as briefly touched on above. The notes and questions should stimulate you to perceive and apply the Word of God from the words of Wisdom, as much as from any other part of Scripture.

As well as the Solomonic collections (10:1–22:16; 25:1–29:27), there are several anonymous sections: chapters 1–9 (the title in 1:1 is probably a general title to the whole book, though some scholars apply it to chapters 1–9 as well); 22:17–24:34, 'Words of Wise Men'; 31:10–31, an acrostic poem on the ideal wife. To these are added two probably foreign sections: 30:1–33 and 31:1–9.

It will be impossible to comment on every proverb. For more detailed introduction and comment, Derek Kidner: *Proverbs* (Tyndale Old Testament Commentaries) will be found useful.

Proverbs: Analysis

1:1–7	**Title, Purpose and Motto**
1:8–9:18	**Discourses on Wisdom**
10:1–22:16	**Proverbs of Solomon: First Collection**
22:17–24:34	**Sayings of the wise**
	22:17–24:22 First collection
	24:23–34 Second collection
25:1–29:27	**Proverbs of Solomon: Hezekiah's collection**
30:1–33	**Sayings of Agur**
31:1–9	**Sayings of King Lemuel**
31:10–31	**Epilogue: The Model Wife**

1:1–7 The beginning of wisdom

These opening seven verses were probably originally an introduction to the first nine chapters of the book, but they form an excellent prologue to the whole collection. Verses 2–6 set out the purpose of the book in a single sentence which introduces, like *dramatis personae*, the concepts that will play their part in the coming chapters. Verse 7 states the underlying theme – the 'axiom' or principle that pervades the whole work.

Verse 2: 'Wisdom' means the competent use of acquired knowledge. 'Instruction' includes the idea of strict educative discipline (see 13:24). 'Insight' is the faculty of discerning judgement that lies at the root of wise action.

Verse 3: 'Wise dealing' is the ability to act with the prudence born of experience and skill, but not, as the second half of the verse shows, out of crafty self-interest. The moral tone of the book – as of Israelite piety as a whole – is summed up in the three words: 'righteousness' (the 'straightness' of God's own character and moral demands); 'justice' (the active implementing of what is righteous in social relations); 'equity' (the personal quality of moral uprightness).

Verse 4: The educational function of the teaching in Proverbs is repeated. 'Prudence' and 'discretion' both contain the idea of shrewdness which elsewhere can mean evil craftiness (e.g. Gen. 3:1).

Verse 5: It is not only the 'simple' or the 'youth' who will gain from the proverbs. Even those already advanced in wisdom can 'increase' in the 'skill' necessary for guidance and direction in daily life (the word 'skill' is linked with a helmsman's steering of a ship).

Verse 7: 'Israel's entire theory of knowledge in a nutshell' (von Rad) (compare 9:10; Job 28:28; Eccl. 12:13; Ps. 111:10). 'The *fear* of the Lord' is not terror. It means taking God seriously in view of his absolute sovereignty and our utter dependence on him. In the context of Israel's covenant with God it meant exclusive devotion and loyalty to him (see Josh. 24:14), pious humility (15:33) and, above all, morally upright behaviour (see Job 28:28). Just as Psalm 19:7–9 includes the 'fear of the Lord' among the things that enlighten man's intelligence, so this motto of the Wisdom literature makes it 'the beginning' of wisdom. 'Beginning' is not just the starting point but the permanent first principle. Negatively (as v. 7b shows), this implies that the ungodly, who do not fear God, have no enduring foundation for wisdom – in intellectual or practical terms. Morally, it subordinates mere knowledge to obedience. Spiritually, it means that knowledge of God and humble submission to him are the only sources of truth.

THOUGHT: How does this 'first principle' of wisdom relate to the 'first and greatest commandment' of the law (Matt. 22:37)?

1:8–33 Wisdom in action

Verses 8,9: The first of many such appeals from parent to son, with the intimacy and urgency of the voice of experience. Following on from the contrast in verse 7, they show that the ways of knowledge or of folly are closely connected to the acceptance or rejection of parental guidance. The attractive beauty of the life guided by such teaching (9) is a repeated theme of the book.

Verses 10–19: Avoid bad company. The father pictures the kind of temptation to which his son is likely to be exposed. The subtleties of it are common to many more forms of temptation than 'robbery with violence'. There is the offer of excitement and 'red-blooded' action (11,12); the lure of quick and easy enrichment (13); the intense pressure of the gang (14) – 'Be one of us!' The sinners' enticement appears to offer a cure for boredom, poverty and loneliness in one easy step. But sin is a destructive deceiver – of tempters and tempted alike. Not only will men of violence perish by violence (18,19, compare Matt. 26:52), they seem quite oblivious of the danger (17, which should probably be translated: 'It doesn't matter if the birds are watching as you strew bait in a net; they will still come for it and get caught, unaware of the danger').

Verses 20–33: Wisdom's reproof. The appeal of wisdom is given greater force by frequent personification throughout the book, with chapter 8 as the most sustained example. This first impression of Wisdom is startling (20,21). We do not find her engaged in polite academic argument in the halls of scholarship, but crying aloud in the street, the markets, the noisy places (better than RSV 'walls', v. 21), the city gates. The wisdom God gives is not the privilege of an intellectual elite, but intended for the practical realities of daily life, for ordinary people going about their shopping, their business and social affairs. That is where God-fearing wisdom really counts.

Verses 24–28 sound callous and heartless, but they are intended to jolt the hearer into a sense of the urgency of the issue. To reject the voice of God's wisdom, to persist in the enjoyment of shallow scepticism and ignorance (22), is to court disaster – which, when it comes, will be irreversible. The consequences of our behaviour may well mock us, but God will not be mocked: we reap what we sow (31, compare Gal. 6:7).

Verses 29,30 show that it is not innocent simple-mindedness but wilful disobedience and perversity that are under judgement. Humble response to God is the only true way to security and peace (33).

PRAYER: Lord, give me your wisdom today in the places where it really counts (verses 20,21).

2 Finding wisdom

The search for wisdom (1–5). Mankind has always had an insatiable desire to increase his knowledge. But what is described here is not a search in a vacuum, or an enquiry into the unknown. This search starts with things already *given* ('my words' and 'my commandments', verse 1). The search is for a right relationship with God through these gifts of revelation – submission to him and intimacy with him (5). A similar balance is found in the teaching of Jesus on the Kingdom of God. On the one hand it is a gift of God which we cannot earn (Matt. 5:3; Mark 10:14,15), and yet we are to strive and search for our experience of it (verse 4 may lie behind Matt. 13:44,45).

The results of the search (6–19), it is again emphasised, are not academic, as though wisdom were simply the fruit of curiosity, but spiritual and moral. Specifically: (*a*) *Moral perception* (6–10). Most moral issues are not black and white. We are faced day by day with a complex range of choices, decisions and responses. Knowing what is right or best is often the hardest part of living as God wants. The answer here is that when our relationship with God is right (5) then the necessary understanding and guidance are given (6) – not by codes and rules, but from within our hearts (10 – compare New Testament teaching on the indwelling Spirit). Verse 9 shows that more than private morality is in view. Those who are saints (8, those who are faithful to the demands of the covenant) seek God's wisdom in the minefield of social and economic relations, too. (*b*) *Moral protection* (11–19). Saints live in a fallen and hostile environment, in which they need a guard as well as a guide. Two representative dangers are mentioned: (*i*) Crooked men (12–15). The synonyms for crookedness (twisted, perverse, devious, dissembling) recur frequently in Proverbs. They present an astute insight into what has been a fundamental flaw in human nature – even at its most respectable – ever since Adam's response to God after the Fall (Gen. 3:8–13). (*ii*) The 'loose woman' (16–19). This *femme fatale* (18,19) appears again in chapters 5, 6 and 7 and will be discussed there.

THOUGHT: 'Whence then comes wisdom? . . . God understands the way to it and he knows its place' (Job 28:20,23).

3 The benefits of wisdom

We move from the protection of wisdom to the positive blessings it gives. 'Loyalty and faithfulness' (3) are words usually attributed to God. The first means enduring covenant love; the second, truth and trustworthiness. As human virtues they are responsive to and imitative of God himself, and imply commitment of life (compare 5–10) and integrity of character (compare 27–35).

Putting God first is the thrust of verses 5–12.

1. At all times (5–8). The mark of fallen man is that he lives by his own wits and cleverness, which is why he ends up in devious perversity. The way of the saint is a healthy distrust of his own insight, and instead wholehearted trust in (5), deference to (6) and fear of (7, see note on 1:7) the Lord. ('Acknowledge', v. 6: the Hebrew is simply 'know'. But really to know the Lord is to accept his will in every situation.) This walk of faith, instead of 'common sense', is incomprehensible to the unbeliever, but it turns out to be 'straight', and it removes the crippling, life-shortening anxiety and stress that underly so much physical illness (8). Peace of mind, security, confidence (see 23–26) are among the greatest and 'healthiest' blessings of faith (compare Matt. 6:25–34).

2. In the good times (9,10). The use of material possessions is a major test of the quality of faith (as the teaching of Jesus showed clearly). 'Honour' is from the same root as 'glory'. It means using wealth in such a way that God is glorified. This is not limited to 'charitable' giving, but includes simple justice in all economic dealings (compare 27,28 and Exod. 22:25–27; Lev. 19:11). Notice 'first-fruits', not 'fag-ends'. Verses 9,10 are a generalisation (compare 1 Sam. 2:30). If it were always or automatically true, then 'God would be not so much honoured, as invested in, by our gifts' (Kidner).

3. In the bad times (11,12). A balance is added to verses 9,10. Faith may be forgotten in prosperity; it can also be destroyed by resentment in adversity. But one who has learned to trust God in *all* his ways (6) can discern his Father's love in discipline as well as bounty (see Heb. 12:5–13 and notice echoes of vs. 6 and 8 in Heb. 12:13). In any case, wisdom, as the fruit of a right relationship with God, is a far better 'investment' than the greatest wealth (13–18).

Verses 19,20, see chapter 8.

Verse 34, compare James 4:6; 1 Peter 5:5.

SUGGESTIONS: Write them on . . . your heart (3). Memorise verses 5–7. Will they be or have they been true of you today?

4 Applied wisdom

From generation to generation (1–9). In passing to his son what he had received from his father, the speaker was discharging an obligation to God (compare Deut. 32:46,47). The teaching function of the family in both faith and conduct is central to the Old and New Testaments (compare Deut. 6:7, 20–25; 11:19; Eph. 6:4; 2 Tim. 1:5, 3:15). Neither Religious Education in school, nor Sunday school and its equivalents can take the place of such family-centred teaching. Christian parents who shift the entire responsibility for their children's instruction to such outside bodies, however good, are abdicating an essential part of God's intention for parenthood.

Verses 7,8: Just like the Kingdom of God in the parables of Jesus (see Matt. 13:44,45) wisdom is of immense value, but needs decisive action and personal appropriation.

Opposite ways (10–19). The ways of the righteous and the wicked are contrasted starkly. Our world of outward appearances is deceptively grey and full of moral relativities. But here, as frequently in Scripture, the truth is seen to be one of total contrasts – as between darkness and light (18,19), or death and life (compare 2:21,22; see Jn. 3:16–21; 1 Jn. 1,2). This is not because the righteous are outwardly perfect or the wicked utterly vile, but because the righteous (here, as throughout the Bible) are those in a right relationship with God through faith and obedience. The wicked, on the other hand, in rejecting this, are on the path to moral and spiritual blindness (19), in which eventually life seems intolerable without evil (16,17). The only way to avoid the end of the road is never to start on it (14,15 – note the pressing urgency).

Body-check (20–27). The moral and spiritual lessons are reviewed in association with parts of the body: ears, eyes, heart (that is, the mind—seat of the will, as well as the memory), mouth and feet. Together they provide a balance between the inner life (especially verse 23; compare Jesus' teaching on the heart, e.g. Mark 7:14–23), and its practical outworking in conduct ('springs of life', that is, what flows out visibly from the inner source). We must guard our hearts *and* our feet (26,27). Notice the dominance of the favourite biblical metaphor for daily living – a pathway (11,12, 18,19, 26,27). The need for guidance, protection, perseverance and progress are some of the ideas associated with it.

THOUGHT: Have a personal 'body-check'. Make use of 4:20–27 alongside Ephesians 6:10–17.

5 Wisdom and sexual temptation

The 'loose woman' introduced in 2:16–19 reappears. There it was said that she is an unfaithful wife heedless of the sanctity of the marriage covenant (2:17). Adultery, therefore, and not fornication or prostitution, is the sin in view in this chapter, and in chapters 6 and 7.

Verses 3–6 vividly contrast the glossy art of seduction with its grim and bitter aftermath, 'in the end' (4): a phrase often used in Proverbs (e.g. 5:11; 14:12,13; 23:31,32), reminding us to look to consequences. In verse 5, 'Sheol', the Old Testament word for the place of the dead, is used as a synonym for death, or the grave. To get entangled with sinners who are already heading for *Sheol* (male – see 1:10–19 – or female, as here) is to experience 'death' even while alive in this world.

Verses 7–14: The legal prohibition of adultery was sanctioned by the death penalty, but the law recognised the difficulty of proof (Deut. 22:22–27; Num. 5:11–31), and it is not known if the penalty was ever applied. The sage, however, applies more practical, economic sanctions, based on the close-knit social structure of Israel. Adultery could lead to the virtual extinction of a man's household. This loss could occur through debts (9,10), physical degeneration (11), dissipated virility (16), social disgrace and loss of status (14; 6:33), financial blackmail (6:26) or attempted compensation to a jealous husband (6:35). Now since, in Old Testament Israel, the privileges of sharing in the covenant community's life in the land of God's blessing largely depended on possession of family and land, to destroy your own household and substance was indeed a kind of self-inflicted death (2:18,19; 5:5, 14, 23; 6:26, 32; 7:23). With such potential results, adultery is for fools only (11, 23).

Verses 15–20: By contrast, the delights of faithful marriage are painted in glowing colours which bloom riotously in the Song of Solomon. Nothing is gained from adultery which cannot be enjoyed, under God's smile, in marriage. There is no answer to verse 20 if verse 19 is true; ('infatuated': literally, saturated, intoxicated). But when sexual intoxication within marriage is allowed to die, the temptation of 'strangers' grows in power.

Verse 21: The sage's advice is not cynically prudential (that is, avoid unpleasant consequences). Behind it stands clear moral accountability to God. We may be clever enough to conceal our sin from men and avoid both judicial and social consequences. But God sees, and there is no escaping the spiritual consequences (22,23).

THOUGHT: Memorise verse 21 as an effective deterrent in times of any sort of temptation.

6 The opposite of wisdom

This chapter is a selection of various follies, followed by another sustained warning against adultery.

Rash promises (1–5). To undertake a pledge on behalf of a friend or neighbour ('stranger' can mean simply someone outside your own family) may be a generous thing to do, but it can land you in trouble, if the friend abuses it or your own fortunes change. Put prudence before pride in such a predicament ('hasten', v. 3 RSV; better, 'humble yourself' – RSV margin). Tell your friend the worst and take prompt action. This is the realistic advice for avoiding ruin.

Laziness (6–11). One of the many suggestive object lessons from nature in the Wisdom Literature, 'the ant' is the harvester ant which uses the short time of harvest to stock up for the year. It doesn't wait to be told (7), and it acts promptly at the right time (8). The sluggard, in contrast, resists all prodding (9) – not with refusal, but with procrastination, 'a little . . . a little . . . a little' (10) – and ends up in the poverty of missed opportunities (11). More about the sluggard in 12:27; 13:4; 19:24; 22:13; 24:30–34; 26:13–16.

The trouble-maker (12–15). The touches of humour here, as in the pictures of the sluggard, should not lighten its serious purpose: the passage exposes the art of sowing discord for the diabolical evil it is. 'A *worthless* person' (12) is literally 'a man of Belial', which implies arrogant disregard for God (compare 1 Sam. 2:12), or any moral principle (1 Kings 21:10), and later became a personal name for the devil (2 Cor. 6:15), the prototype of verse 14.

Abominations (16–19). Here is the 'photographic negative' to the moral 'body-check' of 4:20–27. 'Six . . . seven', like the 'three . . . four' passages in chapter 30, is just a stylistic way of introducing a list. The list is impressive in its vivid brevity. Every phrase is a picture worth reflecting on. It includes sins of attitude as well as action, of thought as well as speech, and culminates with the 'abomination' (something utterly detestable to God) of causing friction among those who should love one another.

More about adultery (20–35). The emphasis here is on the stupidity of it (32), for very obvious reasons (34,35). The RSV margin readings are to be preferred to the text in verses 26a and 30 (compare NIV). Verse 26 emphasises the potential cost of either kind of illicit sexual encounter – prostitution or adultery. Verse 30 points out that a criminal has to pay up even if there is a socially understandable reason for his crime, but adultery lacks any such redeeming feature.

THOUGHT: Have another 'body-check'. How does your conscience react to verses 16–19?

Questions for further study and discussion on Proverbs 1–6

1. How many echoes of these chapters (especially chapter 3) can you find in the Sermon on the Mount?

2. What would you say is the difference between being intelligent and being wise?

3. Why does true knowledge begin with the fear of the Lord (1:7)?

4. How would you integrate the emphasis upon physical well-being (e.g. 3:8, 24; 4:10, 22) into a biblical doctrine of health and healing?

5. How do you decide how much to give to the Lord, and to whom and to what you should give (see note on 3:9)?

6. Make a study (using a concordance) of the word-group 'path', 'way', 'walk' in Scripture. What teaching emerges?

7. Compare 6:14–19 with New Testament passages on love, and the lists of sins to be found in Paul's letters.

8. How can Christian parents best instruct their children in the Christian faith? What advice would you give to parents who want to have family prayers?

7 The protection of wisdom

The lessons of chapters 5 and 6 are now reinforced by a vivid drama of seduction (6–23), sandwiched between urgent warnings to take heed.

It's all very well to ridicule the stupidity of adultery, but the sage knows well enough that the sudden heat of strong temptation evaporates all calm thought about possible consequences. The only protection against it, therefore, is so to engrave the teaching and commandments of the Lord in your heart that they become part of your conscious (2b) and unconscious (3b) life. Otherwise you are as defenceless as the simple youth who in the naïvety of inexperience (7–9) is the victim of an 'attack' so clever that it is irresistible (10–23). The temptation the woman presents is sudden (13), specious (14), flattering (15), sensuous (16,17), sexual (18) and 'safe' (19,20). Any hesitation is suddenly overcome (22) and he is trapped in a snare of folly and sin which is deadly, even if it does not bring him to literal death for, in the thought of Proverbs, one can be in the 'realm of death' through spiritual and moral rejection of God, long before quitting this life (compare 5:5 and Kidner, pages 55,56).

This is an imaginary drama, but the Bible does not spare its real-life heroes either. The stories of David and Bathsheba (2 Sam. 11;12), and Amnon and Tamar (2 Sam. 13) give the proverbial lesson flesh and blood. Prompt use of the feet, responding to convictions of the heart as exhorted in verse 25, is well illustrated in the story of Joseph and Potiphar's wife (Gen. 39:7–12).

THOUGHT: 'These words which I command you this day shall be upon your heart and you shall . . . talk of them when you sit in your house, and when you walk by the way and when you lie down and when you rise' (Deut. 6:7).

8 Wisdom personified

The personification of Wisdom, first encountered in 1:20–33, now reaches a climax all the more powerful for its deliberate contrast with the evil portrayed in chapter 7.

Wisdom's moral appeal (1–9). Some familiar themes recur: that wisdom, however cosmic and eternal, is as down-to-earth as the street corner; that the ways of God's wisdom are *morally* upright; and that effort is needed to seek and acquire it (5,17).

Wisdom's surpassing value (10–21). Wisdom is worth more than the greatest material wealth (10, 11, 19). Why? Because wisdom is the fruit of a right relationship with God (13, compare 1:7; 3:5–10), which is the source of morally upright (13, 20) and personally satisfying (18,19, compare 34,35) living. Authority (15,16) and wealth (18–21) may accrue to the man filled with God's wisdom, but are less important than the righteousness and justice with which he uses both (19,20). So although the Old Testament does include material prosperity among the blessings of God upon those who obey him, there is no unqualified or automatic correlation between piety and plenty.

Wisdom's role in creation (22–31). The personification here is at its most daring, almost exalting wisdom to a 'hypostasis' (that is, an actual heavenly being alongside God). The purpose is to show that wisdom is part of God's own being and activity. It is not optional, not merely desirable, but primary, fundamental to the very existence, structure and maintenance of the universe. If, as such, it brings joy and delight to God himself (30,31), how much more to man (32–36).

But although the beautiful language that speaks of wisdom as a person is, in *this* context, poetic imagery, the New Testament reflection on this passage saw that its deeper meaning was indeed personal. Jesus, the Son of God, was none other than the agent of creation, the pre-existent Wisdom of God, the eternal Word (see John 1:1–14; 1 Cor. 1:24, 30; Col. 1:15–17; 2:3; Heb. 1:1–4; Rev. 3:14).

When the passage is thus related to Christ, it is important to interpret verse 22 correctly. The verb generally means to get, acquire and possess (KJV, NIV), but can sometimes mean to create (RSV, GNB). The Arian heretics used the latter sense to deny the eternal deity of Christ by saying he is a created being. The Jehovah's Witnesses still use this text to argue the same thing. But the first meaning is preferable by far, and gives the sense: 'The Wisdom of God was "there" as part of his character, before ever he began the work of Creation.'

Wisdom's beatitudes (32–36). Echoes of the words of Jesus are not hard to find. Compare verse 35 with John 10:10, 28,29, 14:6.

THOUGHT: How does this passage affect your conception of Jesus Christ?

9 Lady Wisdom and Lady Folly

Here we have the climax and summary of the opening section of the book. The two options open to men are set out under the figure of two banquets – one offered by Lady Wisdom (1–6), the other by Lady Folly (13–18). In between are some of the features of the men who accept invitations to either feast – the wise man, and the scoffer (7–12). The chapter is thus expertly symmetrical, and right at the heart comes the 'motto' with which we started (10).

Verses 1–6: The immediate impression is of spaciousness and ample provision. No one who truly desires wisdom, who accepts what is really *God's* invitation, is turned away or unfilled. 'Seven pillars' is sometimes taken as a reference to seven-pillared pagan temples; sometimes to the seven days of creation. It is probably just a picture of a well-built, orderly house. This Old Testament parable is matched by Jesus' story of the Great Feast (Luke 14:15–24), where the invitation is carried by messengers to the most unlikely people. Just as those who consider themselves healthy will not call a doctor (Matt.9:12), neither will the man of sophisticated arrogance seek the Wisdom that begins with fear of the LORD. Such a person is the 'scoffer' of verses 7–9. Wisdom's feast, like the Great King's, is for the poor and simple who know their own deficiences (4) and in humility wish to have them rectified (6). There is here, as so often in Scripture, a reversal of the world's values and habits. 'The hungry he fills with good things, but the rich he has sent empty away' (Luke 1:53). Ponder, in this connection, Psalm 25:8–14; Micah 6:8; Luke 18:9–14; 1 Corinthians 1:26–31.

Verses 9–11: 'Blessed are the meek' (Matt. 5:5) describes those humble enough always to be teachable. 'For they shall inherit the earth' – a direct quotation from Psalm 37:11, where the context of the rest of the Psalm fits closely with the thought of verse 11 here, and other similar texts in Proverbs.

Verse 12 is a cryptic statement of personal responsibility for the choice we make.

Verses 13–18: The invitation of Folly may sound the same (16, compare 4), but the content of the feast is worthless, satisfying only our fallen perversity (17), and the result inevitable – death, because the folly described is the deliberate, sceptical, scoffing rejection of God, the only source of life. These magnificent nine chapters thus end on a note of deadly earnest. The choice is not just between education and ignorance, but between Life and Death, the fear of the LORD, or self-destruction. Herein lie some of the roots of the urgency of the warnings and appeals that abound in the preaching of Jesus himself.

THOUGHT: 'The fear of the Lord is the beginning of wisdom . . .'

10 Contrasting attitudes

The central section of the book, described as the proverbs of Solomon, runs on to 22:16 and contains some 374 proverbs – an edited selection amounting to some 10 per cent of his total output (compare 1 Kings 4:32)! The contrast with chapters 1–9 is immediately apparent. There we were dealing with lengthy reflections and carefully constructed discourses. Here we are in a thicket of individual sayings, rarely carrying a thought beyond a single verse. The overall concern is the same, however – to contrast the way of wisdom and righteousness with that of folly and wickedness. But it is done by a rapid succession of 'paired snap-shots', each of which calls for a moment's pause and reflection, before passing on to the next. Easier said than done, as each 'snap-shot' captures our attention!

Some classification of the contrasts in this chapter may be attempted:

In speech. Words are important as revealers of what is inside a person. Therefore the contrast of character between the righteous and the wicked is to be seen and heard in their speech (see verses 6, 8, 11, 13,14, 18–21, 31,32). Notice the emphasis upon the dangers and deception of wordiness, of the chattering, babbling, boring effect of the word-mongers who conceal evil intentions behind mind-deadening verbosity. The mass media have magnified the potential danger.

In behaviour. Verses 4,5 repeat a picture found in 6:6–11 – the contrast between diligence and laziness. They are a salutary corrective to any thought that verse 3a excuses us from the hard work of earning our livelihood. There are also portraits of hurtfulness and helpfulness in the way people react to one another in verses 10 and 12 (compare 6:12–19), while the sheer exasperation that comes to those who give any responsibility to the unreliable sluggard is well described in verse 26.

In prospects. The standard of judgement between the two kinds of people is not just the present state of affairs. That may be deceptive at the time (compare 2,3). It is the end result that reveals the difference. See verses 7, 9, 16 (compare Rom. 6:23), 24,25, 27–30. Verse 22 is the key to lasting riches.

THOUGHT: Turn verse 11a into a prayer and a resolve, reflecting on it with the help of Psalm 36:9; Ezekiel 47:1–12; John 4:14, 7:38,39; James 3:3–12.

11 Righteousness and lasting life

This chapter opens many windows on righteousness and its opposite. Remember that 'righteousness', in the Old and New Testaments, means first a right relationship with God who is righteous (through experience of his redemption and covenant 'fear'), and then the responsive outworking of that 'rightness' in practical daily life.

1. Righteousness in economic dealing. Verse 1 states a fundamental biblical principle, found in the Law (e.g. Lev. 19:35,36) and Prophets (Mic. 6:10,11), that economic dishonesty is not just a violation of human codes of practice, but a sin against the Lord himself. Verse 15 echoes the warning of 6:1–5 while verse 18 shows the fickleness of wealth won wickedly. Verse 26 condemns the speculator who deprives people of a commodity in order to profit from higher prices. Some international or multi-national cartels stand under the same judgement. Verses 24,25, dealing with generosity, outline a principle which Paul wove into his teaching on Christian stewardship in 2 Corinthians 9:6–15 – a passage which may well have deliberate echoes of these verses.

2. Righteousness in social life.

(i) Government (10,11). However low may be the standards of common life, people expect integrity from leaders. A double standard, perhaps; but one that is necessary for a stable society.

(ii) Among neighbours (9, 12,13). The slanderer, gossip and talebearer are not only among the most disliked and destructive of people, they are also an abomination to God (6:12–19). The damage they do engulfs themselves (17).

3. Righteousness as a means of deliverance. Life is full of dangers of all kinds. It is asserted repeatedly here that the surest way to safety is an upright life (compare 3, 5,6, 8, 19, 21, 30,31). This can be taken at a temporal level, as saying little more than that 'honesty is the best policy' – which is true, but, as experience proves, not always a guarantee against difficulty or disaster. So a deeper level of truth is hinted at – a spiritual, 'eternal' sense in which righteousness leads to 'life' (19, 30), so that even if verse 18 is not always true in this life, there is a final reckoning (21). At any rate, no hope should be placed in riches by themselves – whether the fruit of wickedness, or even the token of God's blessing. Not what a man has, but what he is, will count on the day of judgement (4, 28).

Note: verse 30. RSV margin is better: *a wise man*, by his influence, wins other men to righteousness (compare Luke 5:10).

TO THINK ABOUT: In what ways do we stand condemned by the standards of this chapter, individually, socially, nationally?

12 The way to security

More about words. (*a*) *Criticism.* (1) How do we react to it? Some are quick to dish out criticisms that may degenerate to insults (16). These are best ignored (which is easier said than done), especially since they can have such cutting, deadly force (18a). But not to tolerate any criticism is plain stupid (1b, 15a,16a). The wise person is prepared both to accept criticism and advice (1a, 15b; 13:10) and to give it (which is often more difficult) where it may be constructive and healing (18b, 25; compare Isa. 50:4; Eph. 4:15).

(*b*) *Truth.* Just as dishonesty in practice is detestable to God, so is lying (17, 19,20, 22). Again, although the purpose is to harm others (6a), the result of habitual falsity is self-destruction – trapped in your own web of deceit (13a). This 'recoil-effect' of sin has been noticed elsewhere (1:18,19; 6:32; 11:17b).

True security. The teaching of 3:23–26 is reinforced in verses 3, 7, 12 (compare 10:25). Mixed metaphors for security are drawn from rooting (compare Ps. 1:3; Jer. 17:7,8) and building. The same two metaphors are used by Paul to describe the security of the believer in Christ (Col. 2:6,7), and the latter by Christ himself, in a way very reminiscent of 10:25 and 12:7 (Matt. 7:24–27). Verse 21 may at first sight appear naive, but it needs to be seen as the true spiritual essence of a deeper truth – the mystery of God's providence, as profoundly expressed in Romans 8:28, and its context.

Once again, the promise of security for the righteous under God's care is not to be taken as an indulgence from hard work in normal daily life (9, 11, 14, 27).

Note: Verse 10. In addition to its simple truth and beauty (illustrated in Exod. 23:4,5; Deut. 22:1; 22:6,7; 25:4;), this verse gives another example of the richness of the Hebrew verb 'to know', which is the verb rendered 'has regard for' (RSV), 'cares for the needs of' (NIV). Was it in Jesus' mind when he said 'I *know* my sheep' (John 10:14)?

THOUGHT: 'In peace I will both lie down and sleep, for thou alone, O Lord, makest me dwell in safety' (Ps. 4:8).

13 Wisdom and wealth

The perversities of wealth. Verse 7 is a dry observation which simply points out that all is not what it seems. There is no direct link between what a man has and what he is, nor between what he actually has and what he would like to be thought of as having. There can be the snobbery of impoverished 'upper classes', or the inverted snobbery of those who call themselves poor but have more wealth than those they would despise as snobs! Verse 8 ironically points out one compensation of poverty: you won't have to face the threat of kidnapping! (8b should read 'a poor man hears no threat', NIV.)

Verse 11 combines our proverb 'easy come; easy go' with a motto fit for any building society. Verse 23 faces the cold fact that even the honest return of hard work can be destroyed by injustice. 'Fallow ground' (RSV) actually means ground freshly prepared for arable farming – a very heavy job. We live in a world twisted by the Fall, in which the unfairness that flaws social life often hits hardest at the weakest (compare Eccl. 9:11). Even apart from the inadequacy of riches as a means of deliverance from final judgement (11:4), they have an inherent fickleness in this life. At the mercy of injustice, accident, inflation, they give false security, as the rich fool discovered too late (Luke 12:13–21), Zacchaeus discovered in time (Luke 19:1–10), but the rich young ruler wouldn't admit to (Luke 18:18–25).

Wisdom: taught and caught. Our earliest lessons are in the family. The first nine chapters are cast in the form of fatherly instruction, and the importance of parental teaching abounds in the whole book. Verse 1 is for the child: to be teachable is the first step in wisdom, but to reject 'home-truths' from your parents is to set course for the godless arrogance of the scoffer in later life. Verse 24 is for the parent: discipline and punishment are not the denial of love, but part of its true expression. To neglect them is to 'hate' the child – not in a conscious, emotional sense, but because of the damage done to the child who will grow up to have an undisciplined, unprincipled life and character.

Wisdom is also learned from the teaching of others. Their experience of life and knowledge of God's Word provide sign-posts to the best in life and help us avoid pitfalls (13,14). But the most powerful influence is that of example. 'You grow like the company you keep', is the message of verse 20.

Notes: Verse 17: Notice again the emphasis on the potential for ill or health that hangs on the truth or falsity of our words. Verse 16: Behaviour shows up character – just as words do (compare 12:23).

THOUGHT: Verse 23 is true of millions of the world's poor. Is this not a challenge to our professed 'righteousness'?

Questions for further study and discussion on Proverbs 7–13

1. Why is adultery such a common and dangerous temptation? Are there any special pressures in modern society? In the light of Proverbs' teaching, how can we best combat this temptation?

2. Make a comparison between 8:8–21 and James 1 and 3:13–18 on the moral results of true wisdom.

3. Study the New Testament references to Christ as the Wisdom of God given in the note on chapter 8. In what respects do they expand your understanding of Jesus?

4. How many parables of Jesus contain echoes of the proverbs of these chapters?

5. What harm can come from too much talking (10:19 and notes)? In what ways can too much talking stop us hearing God?

6. Discuss the obverse of question 5. When can too little talk be a sin?

7. Compare 11:24–28 with 2 Corinthians 8–9. What principles of stewardship emerge?

8. Do you agree with the view of parent-child relationships expressed in 13:24 and elsewhere in Proverbs? Discuss any problems you may have with discipline. What help does Proverbs give?

14 The way to peace and joy

Habits dictate actions. Some proverbs seem trite and obvious, until we notice that they are dealing with matters of habit, making the point that people will do what they habitually do, even in a crisis where the opposite may be required. Thus, a person who often tells lies will do so even in a law court (5b, compare 12:17). The habitual cynic will be incapable of discovering the truth even when he wants to (6a). Gullibility and sensible caution are likewise matters of habit and character (15,16, 18).

Deep in the heart. Verses 10 and 13 show the writer's insight into human emotion. Most of our emotions are shared but there are depths that remain private (10). This experience of something unique and incommunicable is part of the glory and mystery of what it is to be a human person. Verse 13 is a comment on the poignant 'last laugh' of sin upon all present life. Happiness in this life is neither unmixed nor permanent. Only Christ could 'trump' this verse with the gift of *his* joy, which is full, complete and a foretaste of heaven (John 15:11; 1 Pet. 1:8).

Peace of mind. Modern medicine regards as recent discovery what verse 30 observes – that stressful, nerve-ridden living is a cause of physical ill-health, whereas peace of mind has healing potential. This fits with the two warnings against hasty temper and the folly it induces (17, 29). Smouldering resentments (30b) and blazing anger (29b) alike are physically damaging. As spiritual evils they are often mentioned in New Testament lists of sins (Mark 7:22; Rom. 13:13; Gal. 5:20; Eph. 4:31; 1 Pet. 2:1).

Care for the poor. Verse 21 states, as Jesus did, that a mental attitude – contempt or dislike – is sin (compare 20a). Verse 31 goes further and shows why. The poor man is as much a creature in the image of God his Maker as is the rich man (compare 22:2; 29:13). Therefore to treat him unjustly, or even to mock and insult him (17:5), is a sin against the Creator (compare Job 31:15, where this argument is extended to slaves). Notice the progression: 'dislike' (20), 'despise' (21), 'oppress' (31). This introduces a vertical, divine dimension into the vexed issue of 'human rights'. The 'rights of the poor' are not a matter of 'charity' (in the patronising sense) but of our responsibility *to God*, their Creator and ours. Our actions towards them are 'unto the Lord' (compare 19:17). This is true nationally as well as individually (34). Part of the measure of a nation's righteousness is how it treats its poor, or responds to the needs of the poor of the world. Note that these are matters of right and justice, not just altruism.

THOUGHT: Notice how the Bible puts *personal* well-being and *social* responsibility so close together (verses 30,31). Why do we put such a gulf between them?

15 'A word in season'

The art of reply. The reader is used to the emphasis Proverbs lays upon the moral and spiritual importance of our words. The black and white contrasts are echoed by Jesus (Matt. 12:33–37) and James (Jas. 3:2–12). Here the sage reflects on the different ways of answering. There is the *gentle answer* (1), which is infinitely difficult in provocative situations, but does draw the sting out of anger (compare 18). Its opposite (1b) is obvious. Coupled with 18a, it shows that it is people who create quarrels, not circumstances or the subject of the argument. The *perverse answer* (4) belongs to the person who delights in being contrary – a spreader of carping pessimism. The observation that it 'breaks the spirit' is depressingly accurate. The *useful answer* is the mark of the man who thinks before he speaks (28), and who is thus able to say something worthwhile and edifying (2, 7). Not only folly and wickedness frustrate this ideal, but also religious jargon and abuse of spiritual gifts – which led Paul to his preference for 'five words . . . to instruct others' (1 Cor. 14:19, compare 3–5, 12). The *apt answer* is a gift (23) – a source of delight to the speaker and the hearer. The gift is the ability to make an appropriate response – both in words and tone – to any situation. This ability to use wit and humour, comfort, encouragement, truth, rebuke, is worth praying for constantly. The replies of Jesus merit study in this respect (compare also Ps. 19:14; Eph. 4:15; Col. 4:6; 1 Pet. 3:15).

Arrogance and humility. The cynical incorrigibility that is bred by contempt for rebuke is again exposed (5, 10, 12, 20). Such an attitude is self-destructive (32a). Humility, on the other hand, the heart of wisdom, by cultivating a right relationship with God (33), is life-giving (31, compare 14:26,27).

God is all-seeing. (3, 11, 26). The belief in God's ability to see all that goes on (his 'omniscience') was deeply rooted in Israel. It was a logical outcome of belief in a creation filled with moral purpose (Ps. 94:9). The God who sees also knows and judges (compare 5:21). There can be no hiding, for he is also 'omnipresent' (Ps. 139:7–12). Not only actions are visible before him, but the heart and thoughts as well (26, 11: Sheol and Abaddon are synonyms for the world of death and destruction, hidden from all living men, but not from God's sight, compare Amos 9:2, Job 26:6). To act as if he doesn't see (8) is worse than hypocrisy; it is a detestable blasphemy to God (compare Isa. 1:10–17; Jer. 7:8–10).

THOUGHT: Try listening to your own answers.

16 Providence and righteousness

'Man proposes: God disposes'. Solomon's insight into the mystery of Providence may well have been deepened by his awareness of the circumstances of his own birth (2 Sam. 11:1–12:25) and of the varied career of his father David. Men make their plans by deliberate thought (1, 9, 19:21), or by some moral instinct (2a, 21:2) which is fallible and potentially fatal (25, 14:2), or by direct reference to God (33 – the 'lot' was a mechanical means of ascertaining God's will in situations where a simple Yes/No or a selection procedure was required. Its last recorded use is just prior to Pentecost, Acts 1:26; since then the guidance of the Holy Spirit has made it unnecessary). But whatever the method, God has the final word. He 'weighs up' the motives (2), and directs the outcome (9, 33, 21:31), so that his will remains sovereign (19:21). Yet this overall sovereignty of God's purpose does not destroy either a man's freedom in making decisions or his responsibility for their consequences. In particular, as Proverbs so constantly stresses, God's sovereignty does not destroy man's responsibility for the character he forms by his actions and habits. The safest policy, therefore, is regularly to involve God at the outset of every plan (3).

Kingly righteousness. The high ideals of verses 10 and 12–15 were sadly not fulfilled by Solomon towards the end of his reign. These verses point to the standard of righteousness which was required of rulers in Israel whose function it was to carry out the righteous rule of God on earth. Deuteronomy 17:14–20, 1 Samuel 12:13–15 and Psalm 72 are worth studying in this context. As a result of the failure of so many kings the prophets projected into the future their hopes for a truly righteous king (Isa. 9:6,7; 11:1–5; Jer. 23:5,6).

Priorities. Verse 8 is an important balance to the verses extolling the blessings of wealth. If prosperity is at the cost of justice, it is better to be poor. Similarly, better poverty and peace with God than wealth with trouble (15:16). If its enjoyment perverts relationships, better simplicity among friends (15:17; 17:1). If it breeds a dangerous arrogance, better to be lowly and safe (18).

Notes: Verse 4 does not mean God has created people to be wicked, but rather that nothing that happens stands outside God's control or contradicts his overall purpose. 'There are ultimately no loose ends in God's world' (Kidner).

Verse 11: The intensity of God's scrutiny of all human dealings is here extended to the smallest trading transactions. He is the God of the cash register and the shopping basket (compare Lev. 19:36).

THOUGHT: Make verses 12 and 13 the basis of prayer for our political leaders.

17 Justice in the courts

Since righteousness and justice were such prominent attributes of the God of Israel, the demand for integrity and impartiality in Israel's judicial life was rigorous. To pervert justice either by offering (8) or receiving (23) bribes, or to deny it altogether by deliberately unjust verdicts and sentences (15, 26, compare 18:5), was detestable to God. The standards of judicial procedure were clearly set out (compare Exod. 20:16; 23:1–8; Lev. 19:15; Deut. 16:18–20; 2 Chron. 19:6,7), but the failure in practice was bitterly attacked by prophets (Isa. 5:23; Amos 5:12; Mic. 3:9–11). This demand for judicial justice should stimulate Christians to thought and action in the realm of law-making and the processes of law in our society. Justice can never be taken for granted.

Notes: Verse 2. Ability and hard work ought to count for more than privilege.

Verse 3. That God 'weighs' our motives has already been said (16:2). Here the metaphor is changed to testing by fire – the trials of experience which are meant to purify and refine what is worthwhile (compare Jer. 6:27–30; Heb. 12:5–11; Jas. 1:2,3, 12; 1 Pet. 1:6,7).

Verse 5, compare 14:31. Verse 9b, compare 16:28b. Verse 10, compare 15:31. Verse 13, compare Romans 12:17–21, and the life of David after his sin against Uriah for illustration of the proverb. Verse 14 adds to 15:1 the warning that anger, once loosed, quickly becomes as uncontrollable as a flood.

Verse 22, compare 12:25, 14:30, 15:13 and 15. Verse 27, compare 14:17, 15:18.

TO THINK ABOUT: 'Ability and hard work ought to count for more than privilege': do they in your place of work, community, church? If not, is it within your responsibility or power to do anything about it?

18 Using words and finding safety

Still more about words. Every kind of person is observed by the sage, and every kind of use and abuse of words. Often in these proverbs we can 'see' someone known to us. Do we ever see ourselves? There is the *opinionated* fool (2), to whom it is more important to have something to say about everything than to understand anything properly. Some people's conversation is *deceptive,* like deep waters (4); you never know what is really in their mind, in contrast with the clarity and honesty of the wise (4b). The perverted pleasure of malicious *gossiping* is compared to the gourmet's palate (8, see 16:28, 17:9b for the evil results). Exasperating is the *talkative* person who cuts off others with his intrusive 'answers' before they can say what they want (13). The art of *listening,* by contrast, means being fair enough to hear both sides. Verse 17 is obviously drawn from the law-court, but the principle applies to ordinary social life, even more if the 'case' involves misunderstanding between Christians. The critical importance of the matter is again underlined in verse 21 (see also 6,7).

True security (10,11). The 'name of the LORD' means his revealed character. Therefore to know his name, especially his covenant, personal name, 'YAHWEH' (= the LORD in RSV, GNB, NIV), was to know *him.* And to know him was to have experience of his saving and protecting power. Thus, to call on the name of the LORD was to 'run for safety', but only for the person whose deeds showed that he was in a right relationship with God ('the righteous man'). To expect God's protection while living in disobedience, by merely using his name, or his holy place, was a particular sin of Israel exposed by Jeremiah (Jer. 7:1–10). By contrast with the 'strong tower' of God's name the wealth of the rich man is only an 'imaginary' fortress (11). The second line should read as RSV margin and NIV. The two verses combined reverse the usual perceptions of materialistic men who habitually regard the world of property as 'solid' and safe and 'real', and find little meaning, let alone security, in the spiritual realm of trust in God.

Notes: Verse 1 is awkward. It probably refers to a quarrel between friends in which hurtful things are said which may be quite groundless ('pretexts'), and would not even come to mind in ordinary circumstances. Such is the effect of sin even on otherwise happy relationships, however much we may take 17:1 and 18:24b as ideals.

Verse 5, compare the notes on justice on chapter 17.

Verse 14: An accurate observation that physical illness is often more tolerable than prolonged depression.

Verse 22 awaits fuller comment in chapter 31.

THOUGHT: 'Solid joys and lasting treasure none but Zion's children know'.

19 Living in a broken world

More *perversities of wealth* are observed in verses 4, 6. Wealth brings friends – of a sort, as the Prodigal Son found. Poverty is often sharpened by loneliness. These are observations that reflect the harshness of the fallen world (compare 18:23). But is 'bought' friendship real? 18:24 commented on its insincerity, and 19:1 and 22 point to a deeper wealth – personal integrity. Verse 22 suggests that relationships based only on wealth are likely to be fickle and corrupting (compare 21:6) whereas loyalty and truth are intrinsically 'better'.

'God's fault' (3). There is much suffering and calamity in the world that is inexplicable. But there is also a great deal that is directly or indirectly the result of human sin, negligence or 'folly'. Nowhere is the twisted effect of the Fall seen more clearly than in men's quickness to blame God when things go wrong. It was insinuated in Adam's reply: 'The woman, whom *you* gave me . . .' (Gen. 3:12). Christians are not immune to the temptation to react in the same way.

Note again the emphasis on the wickedness of *untruthfulness*, especially when directed at someone else's downfall (5, 9, 28). This shows how concerned the sage was with the social *and* spiritual implications of the Commandments.

Verse 11 adds to earlier proverbs on anger (compare 14:17, 29; 15:18) the opposite virtue of gracious *magnanimity*. 'Glory' is elsewhere translated 'beauty', 'adornment'. There is an attractiveness about patience and the ability to be not easily provoked (compare 1 Cor. 13:4). Verse 19 presents the contrast of one who has a hasty, nasty temper.

Verse 12 (compare 20:2) is a reminder to all who wield some *authority* – in society, in business, in a family. How you treat those beneath you will either produce the sterile paralysis of fear ('lion's growl'), or the productive refreshment of encouragement ('dew').

Verses 13, 14 are more earthly reflections on *marriage*, compare 18:22. 'Dripping of rain' means a leak in the roof which is one of those things that are irritating, but too much trouble to do anything about.

The cartoon imagery continues with the *sluggard* who is too lazy to lift the food to his mouth (24). Comic – but deadly, both in personal hardship (15) and social destructiveness (compare 18:9).

Verse 17 makes two points. First, that God identifies himself with the poor (see Matt. 25:40), which has implications for the motivation of our concern for social justice. Second, that generosity is a matter of 'investment'. That God rewards those who give is not held out as a 'tit-for-tat' incentive, but rather as a statement of spiritual fact. It was likewise taught by Jesus (Matt. 6:1–4, 19–21) and used by Paul as a principle of Christian stewardship (2 Cor. 9:6–15; 1 Tim. 6:17–19).

THOUGHT: How much have you 'loaned' to the Lord in line with verse 17?

20 Values and justice

Honesty and reliability – at a premium. The 'loyalty' and 'faithfulness' of verse 6 are commonly attributed to God. The fact that most men want to be *thought* to possess them shows the ineradicable moral instinct that is part of the image of God in man. The fact that so few *do*, is an indication of the depth of the dye of sin in human life. (These qualities can, in fact, only be possessed and displayed as they are received from God himself – compare 2:5–9). Indeed, the beginning of such character is the personal honesty of verse 9 (compare Job 4:17; Rom. 3:23), by which any form of *self*-righteousness is excluded. The righteousness, however, which starts with such honesty, and continues in integrity, is, through the power of example, the best start a man can give his children (7) – better far than wealth or privilege. For children matter morally. Verse 11 is the truth which lies behind the repeated emphasis on parental guidance and discipline (compare 19:18). It is borne out in Genesis 8:21 (as well as in experience), and shows that God is concerned for children and morally assesses their behaviour.

Laziness again (4, 13). Verse 4 hints at the astonishing optimism of the sluggard. He puts in no work at all, but he's still out looking in case something turns up, when others are reaping the reward of hard work.

Trading injustice. The 'diverse weights' of verses 10 and 23 refers to the deceitful practice of using different weights when buying and selling in order to increase profit and defraud customers. The strong language ('abomination to the Lord') is the negative counterpart to 16:11. It is a rebuke not only to dishonesty in small business or personal money matters, but to the present international system of world trade, with its unfair arrangements, double standards and hidden deceits.

Kingly justice. Verses 2, 8, 26 and 28 reflect the Old Testament, where the king was involved in the practical administration of justice. Hence the stress on the requirement of justice in him personally, compare notes on 16:10 and 12–15.

The folly of revenge. With verse 22 compare 17:13; 24:29; 25:21 and Romans 12:17–21.

Notes: Verse 12, compare 15:3. Verse 17, compare 19:17. Verse 27 – a beautiful description of conscience.

THOUGHT: Don't make your pious promises too quickly (25)!

Questions for further study and discussion on Proverbs 14–20

1. When faced with a big decision how do you decide what to do? What help does Proverbs offer?

2. Is care for the poor and oppressed a matter of charity or duty (ch. 14)? What is the difference? What is your attitude to 'human rights'?

3. With chapter 15 as a starting point, collect as much as you can of biblical teaching on the use of words. Why is it so important?

4. See the notes on chapter 16 headed '*Priorities*'. Compare the thrust of these sayings with the teaching of Jesus and James on the dangers of wealth.

5. What kind of friend do you wish to have/be? See 17:9, 17; 18:24.

6. The Jews trusted in the presence of the Temple, instead of in God. (note on chapter 18). What false securities can Christians find themselves relying on?

7. How do you cope with the temptation to blame God in difficult or painful situations (19:3)?

8. What do you understand by 'personal integrity' (see note on Proverbs 19)?

21 Relating to a sovereign God

The sovereign providence of God is pictured in verse 1. In national or international affairs God is able to use and move the plans and actions of empires as easily as a farmer controls the water that irrigates his land. As illustrations, see Exod. 9:16, Ezra 7:11–28, Isa. 10:5–7, 41:2–4, 45:1–6; Jer. 25:9. How much more, therefore, is his oversight relevant to personal life (2)? Whether, then, it is a matter for personal deliberation (30) or national strategy (31), it is what is in the mind of the Lord that counts. And since the only way to be in tune with the mind of the Lord is to be rightly related to him in faith and conduct, verse 3 logically points out the importance of *doing* righteousness and justice, and the absurdity of relying on religious rituals divorced from morality. God is not impressed by show. The message of this verse, coupled with verse 27 (compare 15:8), was the main-spring of the social vehemence of the prophets (compare Hos. 6:6; Amos 5:21–24; Mic. 6:6–8).

The thought of justice is carried over into the recurring stress on generosity in verses 13 and 26 (compare 19:7), and on judicial integrity in verse 15. Verse 14 should be read as a factual observation, not as a recommendation!

Another twist in the plight of the *sluggard* is noted in 25,26. He has great desires, ambitions and fancies, but lives in a world of constant frustration because of his own idleness. He is at war with himself: his hands *refuse* to work! Verse 26 continues the thought (RSV – 'the wicked' is added; the subject is still the sluggard), but contrasts the active, self-denying generosity which is one of the positive, energetic features of what the Old Testament understands by 'righteousness'.

The quarrelsome wife (9, 19). Wives may retort that these comments are typical male chauvinism and compose their own reciprocal proverbs! One wonders if Solomon spoke from bitter experience among his many wives!

Note: Verse 11, compare 19:25 on the deterrent and educational function of punishment.

TO THINK ABOUT: Look again at what the writer says about justice in action – what does this say about the behaviour of Christians in your community?

22:1–16 Justice and equality

Dangers real and imaginary. Discretion is not only the better part of valour, it is a vital ingredient of life. There is a balance in this chapter between the need to see and avoid *real* dangers (3, 14) and the folly of making *imaginary* dangers an excuse for inaction (13). Some people are simple-mindedly optimistic, perhaps with the best of pious-sounding motives. But they can end up in as many 'thorns and snares' as the deliberately perverse (3b, 5a). Others are innately cautious and see dangers and problems in even the simplest excursion (13). That is a fault not only of the sluggard.

'Created equal'. Verse 2 is one of those 'obvious' deductions from Old Testament creation teaching that has been so callously ignored all through human history, and needed re-emphasising even in the early Christian church (Jas. 2:1–7). Job extended the truth to his slave (Job 31:15). It is interesting that while so much of the Old Testament's teaching on justice for the poor and protection of the weak is based on the writers' experience and theology of *redemption* (see Lev. 19:33–36; Deut. 15:12–15), here in Proverbs it is made a moral implication of *creation* doctrine (compare 14:31, 17:5). Perhaps for that reason verses 8 and 16 can be seen to apply to the world of mankind at large. Injustice, oppression, cruel greed, all bring their own nemesis in the end. The long history of revolution bears out the long-term truth of this, even though verse 7 may crystalise the economic facts of life in the short term. There are those who forecast that the oppressive, self-enriching policies of the wealthy minority of the world population will provoke world-wide conflict that will make verse 16 true on a global scale. Verse 9 repeats the advice of 19:17 and 21:26 and finds an echo in Matthew 6:22, where 'sound' can mean 'generous', and Matthew 20:15.

Childhood discipline. Verse 6 is one of the most quoted proverbs; quoted with hope by parents. Its inner truth is recognised in our expression 'the formative years'. Verse 15 repeats the *moral* factor involved, and locates it where it truly originates – in the heart. Corporal punishment can be horrifically abused. But the abuse does not destroy proper, purposeful and disciplined use – according to this sage, if not according to the more 'progressive' (?) wisdom of our own age (compare 20:11; 23:13,14).

Note: Verse 11 may well have been the basis for the sixth beatitude (Matt. 5:8).

TO THINK ABOUT: What inequalities exist in your community? What should you be doing about them?

22:17–23:14 The words of the wise

'The Words of the Wise' is the title of this sub-section of Proverbs. It separates the two collections of the proverbs of Solomon and runs from 22:17–24:22, with a short appendix, 24:23–34. It has similarities with chapters 1–9 in that the teaching is more connected and grouped into paragraphs, and the didactic 'father-to-son' style is resumed.

In 1923 an Egyptian wisdom text was published, known as *The Teaching of Amenemope*. Many striking similarities exist between this document and Proverbs 22:17–23:14, so much so that scholars argued that one was a translation of the other. Recent research, however, regards Amenemope as older than Proverbs – possibly 12th century BC – and is less certain about 'borrowing' in a strict sense. The suggestion has been made that the 'Words of the Wise' were the work of an Egyptian trained scribe at the court of Solomon who used his memory of the Amenemope text and of other Egyptian wisdom literature as a basis and framework. He was, however, convinced of his own faith in Yahweh, and eager to inculcate it in his readers (22:19). This international character of Wisdom teaching was one of the features of the Solomonic era when Israel made many contacts, trading and cultural, with other nations. The influx of outside ideas and influence could be 'disinfected' of paganism and idolatry and turned to good use. Sadly, they were often not 'disinfected' – even in Solomon's own lifetime (1 Kings 11). The people of God have nothing to *fear* from surrounding, pagan culture. But their use of it needs to be discriminating and constantly subjected to the criteria of faith and righteousness (compare 23:17).

The ancient landmarks (22:28; 23:10) were the boundary stones marking off the division of the land among clans and families (Josh. 13–19). To pinch land by shifting the boundary stones was a crime in all ancient societies. In Israel it was the more heinous because the land was the gift of the Lord to be shared by all Israel. It was an inalienable spiritual inheritance, over which the Lord retained the ultimate right of ownership (Lev. 25:23). Thus, to move a boundary-stone was the epitome of oppressive wickedness (see Deut. 27:17; Job 24:2,3; Hos. 5:10). The redeeming justice of God is invoked on behalf of the victims (11, see 22:23). 'Redeemer' here means the strong kinsman who is able to vindicate and deliver his oppressed brother (compare Lev. 25:25; Ruth 3:12,13; Isa. 43:1).

The strains of snobbery (23:1–8) is a satire on the person who wheedles his way into the company of the powerful or the wealthy. He cannot be at ease (2–5), and cannot even enjoy the favours he is grudgingly given (6–8).

THOUGHT: If the words of scripture are to be 'ready on your lips' (18), they have to be deep in the heart, which makes work for the mind (17).

23:15–24:7 The dangers of envy and drunkenness

Happy families. The result of parental discipline – and its joyful reward – is the growth of upright character, of maturity and wisdom in the child. Thus verses 15,19 and 22–25 off-set the hard realism of verses 13,14. The motivation and the dividend of living by the fifth commandment and Ephesians 6:1–4 are thus portrayed as abundant rejoicing – far removed from the caricature of authoritarianism or repression.

Misplaced envy. Being sinners ourselves, all of us, there is a natural tendency both to admire and resent those who 'sin big' and appear to profit by it. It was a mood that gripped the Psalmists, too. Psalm 73 is an extended meditation on the problem. But to indulge such envy and fretfulness is self-destructive and 'tends only to evil' (Ps. 37:8). In order to neutralise it, the sage advises the reader to think ahead to the consequences of the sin he envies (23:18; 24:20; compare Pss. 37:2, 9; 73:17–20), and to stabilise his heart in the fear of the Lord (23:17). The danger is that the harbouring of such envy of sinners may lead to emulation of their habits and vices. This is suggested by the way 23:17, 18 and 24:1,2 'sandwich' a section mainly concerned with the lascivious pleasures of grand-scale sinners whom others envy: gluttony (23:20,21), lust (23:26,27) and drunkenness (23:29–35).

The drunk (23:29–35). The sage is as acutely observant of this character as of the sluggard and, as in his pictures of laziness, he uses touches of humour. But the cartoon effect serves a very serious purpose, for it describes something which in real life is very unfunny indeed – the degenerative disease of alcoholism. Verse 31 pictures the initial fascination of strong drink, followed by its bitter end (32). The physical and mental derangement and absurd confusion are likened to sea-sickness (33,34); the belligerent swagger, the actual bodily harm, the hazy stupor, and finally the belief that the only solution is another drink (35), are all captured like photographic stills. The result? Woe, sorrow, strife, complaining, injury and ugliness (29). Still envious?

Note: 24:7 – 'the gate' was the place of all serious debate, particularly on legal matters.

THOUGHT: **'I was envious of the arrogant . . .**
But when I thought how to understand this,
it seemed to me a wearisome task,
until I went into the sanctuary of God;
then I perceived their end.' (Ps. 73:3, 16,17)

24:8–34 Strength of character

Even apart from God's judgement, men have ways of meting out their own disapproval, either by destroying a reputation, or by ostracism (8,9).

The tests of character (10–12). It is pointless claiming to be strong if your strength is never tested. Faith in God's power and guidance only begin to count when circumstances appear to contradict them. Verse 11 probably refers to the imminent execution of someone when evidence could have been given to save him. It may metaphorically include a preparedness to help those in need even if getting involved is inconvenient and possibly dangerous. To say, 'It's not my business' or, 'It's not my fault', is an excuse that does not fool 'the God who sees' (12). We may not be responsible for (that is, guilty of causing) the plight of others, but we are still held responsible to God for them as persons. The Good Samaritan perceived this, while those who should have realised it passed by, doubtless with precisely the above excuses in their minds. The last four lines of verse 12 again introduce the vertical dimension of God's oversight. We are answerable to him in the discharge of our responsibility for others. This is the biblical basis of a sound view of human rights.

Present pleasure and future security. Verses 13 and 14 go together. The thought is that wisdom has a dual benefit. It can be enjoyed with pleasure, satisfaction and nourishment *now*, like honey; but unlike the transience of so much that is 'sweet', its blessings are permanent. Verse 14b is vague, but it points to a hope beyond this life that later revelation gave content to.

Resist gloating (17,18, compare 29). These verses relate to personal animosities, not the collective destruction of the wicked or defeat of national enemies (though, even on that larger scale, the response of the man of God is to share the pain of God in judgement – as Jeremiah wept for Jerusalem, Jer. 9:1, as did Jesus, Luke 19:41–44, as Abraham interceded for Sodom, Gen. 18:22–33, in contrast to Jonah's anger when Nineveh was spared, Jon. 4). Verse 18 is not cynically saying that your gloating may shorten your enemy's suffering, but rather that the sin of your arrogant and self-righteous rejoicing is likely to be worse than whatever has caused your enemy to fall.

Verses 23–34 are a short appendix of further anonymous proverbs. Note the emphasis again on judicial integrity, both in administration of the law (23–25) and in witness (28,29).

Verse 27: 'Build your house' probably means 'raise your family'. The verse advises a responsible and prudent approach to marriage and home.

THOUGHT: Are you facing a 'day of adversity'? Where will your strength come from? Remember 2 Corinthians 12:5–10.

25 The rights of authority

The next section (25:1–29:27) is a further collection of the proverbs of Solomon, edited around 700 BC by the scribes of King Hezekiah (715–687 BC).

King and court (2–7). The sovereign ways of God are beyond the probing of finite minds (compare Deut. 29:29; Isa. 40:13), but the king is there to be the eyes and ears of God's righteousness in society. Authority has the right of enquiry, though the wickedness of a police-state tyranny is far from the thought of the proverb. Authority itself needs to be subject to moral refining (4), susceptible as it is to corruption (5) and power-seeking (6, compare Jesus' advice, Luke 14:7–11). The role of God's people in a secular society to act as a morally refining force upon the 'court' – that is, whatever institutions or groups exercise power and authority – is thus clear and urgent.

Hasty judgement (8–10). To take instant action on appearances may be bitterly regretted. How many public quarrels could be avoided if we paused to ask about motives, to hear both sides (compare 18:17), to talk privately? The teaching of Jesus in Matthew 18:15–17 reinforces this (compare 1 Cor. 6:1–6).

Words again. The art and beauty of fitting words, especially words of reproof wisely heeded (11,12); the powerful effect of patience and gentleness (15); the refreshment of good news (25); the insensitivity of attempts at jollying (20); the violence of lying (18); the frustrating emptiness of unfulfilled promises (14): all are presented in striking metaphors. Expressing grief can be a source of warmth and comfort against the blast of tragedy. To force someone to 'cheer up' is to remove even that 'garment'.

'Enough is enough' is the point of verse 16, which is applied to considerate neighbourliness in verse 17, but also to material things in 30:8,9.

Trustworthiness provides emotional refreshment (13). The pain and insecurity of its opposite is felt most deeply when a faithful friend is needed (19, compare 26:6). Worst of all is one who has a reputation for righteousness but succumbs to wickedness – consciously or unconsciously. People rely on a name and reputation, just as the thirsty trust a spring. To be poisoned in good faith is doubly tragic. Those with a teaching or leadership responsibility in the church need to keep watch on the wholesomeness of their output (compare James 3:1).

Coals for conscience (21,22). These verses, quoted in Romans 12:20, are clear in teaching positive kindness to those who 'despitefully use you' (see Matt. 5:43–47). The 'coals of fire' should be understood as the fire of conscience and *not* as the fire of God's judgement.

THOUGHT: Are you and your Christian community exerting any purifying influence on the political authority within your reach?

26 The fool, the sluggard and the trouble-maker

Three types that we have already met are presented in close-up for our warning: the fool (1–12), the sluggard (13–16) and the trouble-maker (17–28).

We need to remember that *the fool* in Proverbs is not an idiot or simpleton. These verses are not callous sarcasm at the expense of the unintelligent. Just as wisdom is the outworking of fear of the Lord, so folly is a spiritual condition. It is rejection of God, a wilful persistence in arrogance (scoffing) and disobedience. Such people may be found in positions of honour, but there is an incongruity and futility about that (1, 8). They may be entrusted or employed, but both alike are dangerous (6, 10). They may be chastened, by man or by circumstances (3) but, humanly speaking, they are incorrigible (11, compare 27:22). Verses 4 and 5 are not contradictory. Each is appropriate, depending on the circumstances. As Paul found, some arguments are futile and destructive, to be avoided altogether (compare 2 Tim. 2:23; Prov. 29:9), but on other occasions, when an important principle or the truth of the gospel is under attack, then an answer has to be made (compare 2 Cor. 11:1–12:11; Gal. 1:6–9; 2 Tim. 2:25).

The one point that is added to earlier proverbs about *the sluggard* is that laziness breeds its own rationalised self-defences (16), which the lazy person eventually comes to believe. Christians are not immune – though our excuses may be spiritualised as well.

We met the interfering *busybody* earlier (6:12–19). Whereas we look for the causes of strife in circumstances, issues, 'things', Proverbs pinpoints as the 'kindling' (21) the personal factor – the whispering words and hatred. Verses 18 and 19 not only warn against the dangers of harmful practical jokes, but also present another example of Proverbs' dislike of 'escape clauses' (Kidner) to cover our negligence or thoughtlessness; compare 24:12: 'I never knew', or here: 'I meant no harm, I was only joking.'

THOUGHT: 'A flattering mouth works ruin' (28).

Questions for further study and discussion on Proverbs 21–26

1. If God is omnipotent in his providence, what room is there for personal choice and planning (21:20, 31)?

2. 'The lazy man . . . is greedy to get, while the godly love to give' (21:26 Living Bible). How can we avoid being 'greedy to get'? In what ways can we practice generosity?

3. What varieties of feeble excuse are made the pretext for spiritual or evangelistic laziness (22:13)?

4. What governs your choice of what to watch, read and listen to (see note on 22:17–23:14)?

5. Meditate on the application of 24:1 to your own life, with the help of Psalms 37 and 73.

6. In what ways has the 'burden of knowledge' (via modern media) affected our responsibility for the rest of the world (24:12)?

7. What kind of arguments should be avoided, and what kind taken up (26:4,5)?

8. We are aware of many injustices. Is there one area in particular which you as a group could focus upon for study and prayer? Is there any action you can take?

27 Coping with praise

Verse 1 is alluded to in James 4:13–5:6 as a warning against the insecurity of material wealth – especially if founded on injustice, and may well lie behind Jesus' parable of the Rich Fool (Luke 12:16–21), though Jesus actually quotes verse 1b as a bulwark against faithless anxiety (Matt. 6:34). Hard work in preparation for 'tomorrow' is, however, not excluded (23–27, compare 24:27, 28:19).

Praise. The advice of verse 2 is turned into a test in verse 21. To be the object of praise is a sterner test than to be the victim of contempt. Whether the praise is deserved or not, sincerely meant or flattery, it acts as a 'crucible', inasmuch as it tests the loyalty of the heart to God, the reality of our humility before him and the sincerity of our profession that all we have and are comes from him. The giving and receiving of praise within a Christian fellowship needs care, therefore. There is great value in the word of encouragement and gratitude (as in most of Paul's letters). But a fine line divides this from sugary praise that 'puffs up' and can mushroom into the adulation and hero-worship that bedevils many Christian movements. Note the warnings of Jesus in John 12:43 and Matthew 6:2, 7, 16.

Love-wounds (5,6). The opposite of praise – rebuke – is also a test of love. Much has already been said in Proverbs on the need to be willing to *accept* criticism and reproof. Here the thought is that love may demand a willingness to *give* rebuke. 'Hidden love' (5b) means love which fails to show itself by speaking the truth (5a). The 'wound' of a friend, is given out of integrity and truth ('faithful', 6a), and will ultimately be healing.

Verse 7 pinpoints the distortions that are wreaked in human life and judgement by *both* excess of wealth *and* acute poverty. One is nauseating (see 28:16), the other reduces everything to a desperation that makes even abominations seem necessary and desirable (see 30:9b).

Verse 14 – a favourite text among my Christian friends at a residential college! Like much else in Proverbs it captures principles of consideration and neighbourliness that lie beyond the scope of laws or codes.

Verse 19: this cryptic proverb (literally, 'As the water the face to the face, so the heart of a man to the man') probably means that it is what goes on in your heart and mind that truly reflects what you are, and not the opinions others may have of you (compare verse 21). If God looks on the heart (see note on 15:3, 11, 26), we ought also to be concerned with more than our own external image.

THOUGHT: what mirror are you using to see yourself in?

28 Private conscience and public evil

Private conscience. Verse 1 pictures the haunted conscience of the wicked and contrasts it with the confidence of the man whose conscience is right with God. The contrast is deepened in verse 13 (compare the classic Old Testament exposition of this in Ps. 32, and the way 1 John 1:8,9 can add God's justice to his mercy, in the light of the propitiation of Jesus' blood), and strengthened in verse 14. Unconfessed sin soon hardens the conscience till it feels no guilt (compare 30:20). Verse 17 probably also has reference to the 'burden' of conscience on the murderer, but also prohibits interfering with the course of the law (compare Num. 35:31–33).

Public evil. There is an emphasis in this chapter and in chapter 29 on the connection between social injustice and institutional wickedness at the top. Verse 2 was abundantly illustrated in the history of the last decades of the Northern Kingdom of Israel, when kings followed one another in rapid succession, in coup after coup, while the country fell apart morally and socially, and eventually fell altogether before Assyria in 721 BC. All this had been witnessed by Hezekiah's generation in Judah (see 2 Kings 15–17). Verse 3 is well illustrated by the sorry modern spectacle of leaders in some of the poorest countries of the Third World exploiting their own poor. Often the ruling elite may have come from a poor background themselves. Their oppression has thus the added bitterness of betrayal – just as when rain which is expected to restore and fertilise the crops beats and destroys them.

Another astute observation, which the modern economic scene bears out, is the way in which wealth and institutional evil dull the thinking and produce their own self-righteous justification, whereas poverty has its own educative incentive (5, 11, 16a). Chapter 28:5 should be coupled with 29:7. It is the privilege of those who know and seek the Lord to have insight into the true nature of justice. Such knowledge brings its responsibility – to defend the 'rights of the poor'. As the Old Testament law re-echoes this theme repeatedly, there is an appropriate emphasis on familiarity with and observance of the law (4, 7, 9).

As often, the teaching of Jesus can be seen to echo themes in Proverbs: (for example, verse 10, compare Matt. 18:6; verse 22, compare Matt. 6:19–24; verse 24, compare Matt. 15:3–6).

THOUGHT: Verse 21b: temptations don't have to be very big to succeed.

29 A just society

Verse 1 is a general truth which Scripture often presents as a warning against resisting the word of God (see Ps. 95:7–11; Matt. 23:37,38; Heb. 12:25), but since the context here highlights the responsibility of rulers, it is worth noting the royal illustrations of the verse – for example, Pharaoh, Saul, Jehoiakim (Jer. 36), Herod (Mark 6:20). The implications for rulers, righteous or otherwise, are expanded in verses 4, 12, 14. It is worth noting, as a corrective to our habit of thought, that whereas we tend to measure social righteousness and stability in what we label 'moral' terms (that is, mainly matters of sexual or familial morality), Proverbs, without in the least minimising those issues, measures it in terms of economic justice. Thus institutionalised bribery and corruption will render a country endemically unstable (4), while 'the test of a man in power, and his hidden strength, is the extent to which he keeps faith with those who can put least pressure on him' (14, Kidner). Such a man will 'know', that is, 'look after the interests of' (compare 12:10), the poor and weak in society. Again, the law is relevant here. It is the man or group who is steeped in the spirit of the Old Testament law, with its demand for economic and social fairness, who can exercise that prophetic vision (18) without which society runs amok. The Wisdom writer thus unites his own voice with that of the law and the prophets (compare Hos. 4:1–6). At the same time, however, such a man or group realises that ultimately the Lord himself is the source and giver of all right and justice (26). This is both a caution against undue optimism in human authority, and an encouragement to surround all social concern and involvement with prayer.

Familiar themes recur in this final chapter of Solomon's proverbs: assorted 'snares' – flattery (5), wickedness (6), pride (23), fear of man (25a); arrogance and temper (8,9, 11, 20, 22); violent persecution of the righteous (10, 27); discipline (15, 17, 19, 21). The translation 'heir' (21b) is doubtful. The word is obscure, but may mean 'a moral weakling'. Verse 13, compare notes on 14:21, 31 and 22:2.

TO THINK OVER: What does this chapter say to the society in which you live?

30 The words of Agur

The collection of proverbs ends with three short appendages: the words of Agur, the words of Lemuel, and an anonymous poem in praise of a good wife (31:10–31).

The word 'Massa' in the title of chapters 30 and 31 means 'an oracle' (thus NIV). But RSV takes it as the proper name of an Ishmaelite clan. If this is the true sense, then Agur and Lemuel were probably of Arab race, and these chapters bear witness to the international character of Wisdom in Israel (compare 1 Kings 4:29–34).

Verse 1b. Either Ithiel and Ucal were pupils of Agur, or the Hebrew can be revocalised to make an exclamation of weakness which fits with the mood of verse 2 (see NIV margin). There can be no certainty, but the first is probably best.

Agur was a man of honest humility (2,3) which stemmed from a clear vision of God's transcendence (4, compare Job 38) coupled with total trust in the truth, power (5) and sufficiency (6) of God's revealed word. His attitude is thus wholly at one with the motto of Proverbs: fear of the Lord as the principle of wisdom. This foundation leads him to a balanced view of life (7–9) which, like 25:16 and 27:7, enshrines the biblical goal of 'enough'. The best commentary on verse 9a is Deuteronomy 8:11–20 coupled with 1 Timothy 6:6–10. Verse 9b shows that poverty, while being an understandable motive for theft, does not neutralise it as a moral and spiritual evil.

The rest of Agur's sayings are mostly grouped into fours, but the 'three . . . four' device gives them the feel of 'a few examples that could be added to if you like' and not of complete lists.

Verses 11–14. Four snap-shots of evil arrogance: childhood impudence (11, 17 – where the penalty, with its implication of lack of burial, appears to reach beyond death), self-righteousness (12), snobbery (13), exploitation (14).

Verses 15,16. The root of the sin of verse 14 is here unearthed as insatiable greed. Covetousness is idolatry (Col. 3:5, compare 9); it also is the parent of social blood-sucking (15, see Mic. 2:2).

Verse 20. The point is probably that sin can become so natural and acceptable to the one who sins that the conscience is effectively silenced. If adultery can become as natural as eating, how much more the 'lesser' sins.

The remaining three groups of four are skilful observations, given without moralising. The reader is left to come to his own conclusion about what is obnoxious (21–23), the superiority of wits over bulk (24–28), and inherent majesty (29–31). The gentle humility of the author surfaces again in his concluding, vivid verses (32,33).

THOUGHT: Are verses 8,9 a valid prayer for a Christian? Are there New Testament parallels?

31 A good king and a good wife

The Words of Lemuel (1–9): the wise advice of a king's mother, who appeals to both his filial love and the fact that she has dedicated him to God (2). The advice is a warning and an encouragement. The warning is against dissipating the energy and clear-thinking he will need as a king either in sexual promiscuity (3, a particularly 'available' temptation to kings – compare Solomon) or in drunkenness (4). That drink dulls the senses is noted without comment (6,7), but that is the last thing a legislator and judge needs (5). The encouragement is to fulfil the ideals of righteous kingship – protection of the rights of the powerless who have no 'loud voice' in society, of the destitute, poor and needy (8, 9). We note once again that the glory of kingship has nothing to do with external pomp and majesty, but with moral integrity and social justice (see notes on chapters 16 and 20). The same applies to all forms of institutional authority and to those who exercise it.

A fine wife (10–31). This is an alphabetic poem (acrostic) where each verse begins with a successive letter of the Hebrew alphabet. It is a resplendent counterweight to the scattered sniping at less worthy wives in the proverbs of Solomon, as well as to the more concentrated vehemence against the adulteress. On the one hand it gives the lie to the view that womenfolk in Israel were little more than the chattel property of the men, but on the other hand it is hardly typical of the majority of ordinary wives. For this woman is obviously part of a family of considerable substance, with servants (15), investment capital (16) and trading interests (18, 24) and is able to afford the best ('scarlet', 21). Nevertheless, the underlying character of the woman is 'ordinary' in that it is available to all – her conscientious hard work (13, 17, 27), her trust and trustworthiness as regards her husband (11,12, 28,29), her care and provision for the household (21, 27), her generosity (20) and kindness (26). But the climax of her qualities – that which undergirds them and which is without question to be emulated – is her fear of the Lord (30). She thus comes as a most fitting epilogue to a book which has had that as its motto.

This woman's generosity (20) is all the more remarkable in view of her rank in the 'upper classes'. It stands in stark contrast to the behaviour of the upper class women who were observed and condemned by Amos (4:1) and Isaiah (3:16–24).

CHALLENGE: 'Open your mouth, judge righteously, maintain the rights of the poor and needy' (9).

Questions for further study and discussion on Proverbs 27–31

1. When you are doing routine jobs what thoughts does your mind drift into? What does this reveal (see notes on 27:19)? Have you discovered for yourself, or read or heard of ways of altering your habits of thought? What does Proverbs suggest? (Compare Brother Lawrence, *The Practice of the Presence of God*.)

2. What factors make the difference between genuine encouragement and dangerous flattery (27:21)?

3. 28:5 and 29:7 say that the righteous understand and care about justice. Do you? Is Christian lack of concern for social justice due simply to ignorance about it? If so, who is to blame?

4. What principles can you draw from chapters 28, 29 and 31:8, 9 that the Christian church should be advocating to those in positions of power in society?

5. Read 30:6. In what ways do we or others do this?

6. What does 31:10–31 contribute to overall biblical teaching on family life?

7. Discuss together times when you have discovered the truth, power and sufficiency of God's word.

8. How would you summarise the 'teaching of Proverbs'? How apt a summary is 'the fear of the Lord'? If you had to select one thing which has most challenged you, what would it be?

Ecclesiastes: Introduction

The title is the Greek translation of the Hebrew *Qoheleth*. This may mean 'one who addresses the assembly' though he does it more as a wise counsellor (compare 12:9,10) than as a 'Preacher' – the English sub-title. We shall preserve his anonymity by simply calling him 'the author'. Almost all scholars, including conservative ones, regard the word as probably post-exilic, that is, among the later books of the Old Testament. The older traditional view that Solomon wrote it is based on 1:1, but 1:16 and 2:9 imply that many others had been king before, which was not true of Solomon. Yet who could have 'surpassed' Solomon? The claim to royalty (1:12 – curiously past tense) and the shades of Solomon are most probably an accepted literary device, partly to associate the work with the Wisdom genre, of which Solomon was 'patron saint', and partly to highlight the message of the first two chapters – after which the royal glow fades out.

The problem of the interpretation of the book is discussed in the first section of the commentary. The reader would profit from a cursory read through the whole book of Ecclesiastes, to get the 'feel' of it, before working through the sections. The GNB is excellent for this purpose (though RSV continues to be the basis for the notes).

Ecclesiastes: Analysis

The following analysis is somewhat arbitrary since, apart from the introductory and concluding sections, the book has no clearly defined structure. It is more like a 'theme and variations' than a classical symphony.

1:1–11	**Introduction of author and theme**
1:12–3:22	**Explorations into the meaning of life**
4:1–6:12	**Assorted evils 'under the sun'**
7:1–9:18	**Fruits and frustrations of wisdom**
10:1–20	**An interlude of proverbs**
11:1–12:14	**Concluding advice and 'signature'**

1:1–11 Faith and futility

The author plunges us without ceremony under the cold shower of his text: 'All is vanity!' (2). The word means 'empty, useless'. As it reverberates through the book it gathers the implication 'pointless and frustrating'. Nature and history alike are a meaningless round of repetition (4–11). What point can there be then in human life and work (3)?

How can such a book, with its cynical questions and disturbing answers be part of the canon of Scripture? How are we to cope with its pessimism and nihilism? There are those who regard it as a wholly secular, humanistic work, not at all inspired by the Holy Spirit, which has got into the canon by accident. But that is to abandon it rather than to interpret it.

The traditional Jewish interpretation, which became the mainstream Christian understanding, was that it was intended to expose the vanity of all 'wordly' pursuits ('under the sun') and thus direct the mind and spirit to the higher things of God himself. Such a view easily fitted with a false world-denying form of Christianity. This stance could be modified to see the book's purpose as exposing the pointlessness of life *without God*. This has been further refined by G. S. Hendry (*New Bible Commentary Revised* pp. 570f.) and D. F. Kidner (*A Time to Mourn and a Time to Dance* – his excellent commentary on Ecclesiastes), as a case of 'hidden agenda'. The author, himself a man of faith, puts himself in the shoes of the unbeliever, and describes life *hypothetically*; 'this is what it must be like for a man whose frame of reference is bounded by time and space'. The purpose is thus 'pre-evangelistic', to strip away the illusions down to bedrock, so that the reader, by faith in God's judgement, can begin a rebuilding.

The trouble is that the book itself really gives no explicit clue that it is such a piece of ventriloquism. The author seems as convinced of his pessimism as he is of his faith in a moral, sovereign creator, God. The two co-exist in tension, and the faith does not really *answer* the charge of 'vanity', which persists right up to the last expression of faith in ch. 12. Faith, for the author, is not so much a secret computer that has the answers, as a filing tray marked 'Pending'.

Ecclesiastes pushes to its uncomfortable limit a tension, found also in Proverbs, between a vision of the world as it ought to be, with righteousness prospering and wickedness confounded, and observation of the world as it is, with its injustice and absurdities. The first is the voice of faith in the character and promises of God; the second is the voice of harsh experience. And it is the strength with which the faith in God's revelation is held that produces the agony over the state of the world. The world poses no great *moral* problem for the atheist (why should it be other than it is?), or for the polytheist (what else can you expect with a chaos of rival gods?). But for one who accepts the revelation of *one, good, sovereign* God, it *is* an enigma.

The book is an honest assessment of the world as fallen, as under the curse of God. The futility of life is precisely what Gen. 3 sentenced the world to. The earth mediates God's judgement upon man.

Within the limits of the revelation he had received, this is an agonised, but valid, comment by a man of faith on the state of the world since the Fall. But of course it is not an adequate or final comment. For that we need the rest of God's revelation in Scripture, and in particular two great truths of the New Testament. First, that the God the writer believed in would himself *enter* this twisted world and suffer its worst wickedness. He, the just, would die for the unjust. In the Incarnation and on the Cross God accepted, experienced, and dealt with the ruin of the Fall, turning apparent futility and defeat to victory. Second, that the fruit of that victory would ultimately be the reversal of the Fall, the lifting of the curse for *all* creation. Romans 8:18–25 is the key and answer to Ecclesiastes. Paul, too, sees nature as subjected to frustration/vanity. Since he uses the same Greek word as the Greek translation of the Old Testament uses for 'vanity' in Ecclesiastes, he very probably had that book in mind. But his vision is of nature redeemed and restored, upon the completion of the redemption of mankind. We can now look forward to 'new heavens and a new earth where righteousness dwells' (compare 2 Pet. 3:13). This is the 'eschatological' perspective that our author lacked and which, for the Christian, gives meaning to the present.

1:12–2:11 A laboratory of life

The author plans to conduct a full-scale 'scientific' enquiry into life on earth (13). To do so, he speaks in the guise of Solomon (12) as one who had unbounded opportunity to sample every aspect of life. The 'research project' is no less than 'all that is done under heaven', and the preliminary verdict is given in 13b–15. Note that the author is no atheist. He sees God as the sovereign director even of the sorry state of the world. Verse 15 is probably a way of saying that the whole quest is limited both by 'circumstances beyond our control' and by our own finitude.

The 'experiments' (1:16–2:10) cover a very varied range of human experience and endeavour. The author throws himself into every human condition – but always with a degree of detachment – the 'scientific objectivity' he needs in order to make his assessment. This is the point of the phrase 'my mind still guiding me' (2:3), even when he is sampling drunken dissipation.

First, he rises to the heights of learning and intellectual prowess (1:16). But this only increases his awareness of the sharpness of the enigmas of life (18). Knowledge can be a burden. 'The more you know, the more it hurts' (GNB). So he swings to its opposite – the world of irrationality and folly (1:17b, 2:3b). This is one of the several places where the author strikes a very 'modern' note. Our age has seen the flight from rationality, into the cult of the meaningless, the absurd, the weird – in art, literature and music. Then he tries 'hedonism' – the pursuit of sheer pleasure (2:1–3), but finds this at best meaningless (because it leads to nowhere beyond itself), and at worst, ending up in cynicism ('mad' laughter). So he turns from that dead-end to an apparently productive road – creative activism and hard work (2:4–6). This, he admits (10b), did give him satisfaction in the *doing* of it, and it had the bonus of aesthetic appreciation, and abundant wealth (7,8). But when he *thinks* about it (11), his verdict has to be the same: empty in itself, and with no lasting meaning; no lasting profit.

THOUGHT: Is frantic Christian activism any better?

2:12–26 Wisdom and work

A fuller reflection on his 'experiments' is called for, knowing that no one will have a greater opportunity for such enquiry after 'Solomon' (12b). Was his preliminary assessment not too harsh? Surely there is a value and joy in a life of useful work? The author is not going to deny this (compare 24,25), but what he cannot see is that it has any ultimate value or profit beyond the immediate satisfaction it gives. Death sees to that.

Before introducing death, however, the author quotes two proverbs (13, 14a) extolling wisdom over against folly. He agrees; they *must* be true; they are axiomatic – and yet death seems to make nonsense of them. Death deals a double blow. It appears to rob a man's *life* of any dignity (15,16), for what is it worth to be wise if you die like a fool? And it robs a man's *work* of any point or profit (18–23). You have to leave whatever you achieve to someone who may destroy it (19), and will not deserve it (21). The author is brutally honest about death. There is no romantic euphemism. If values depend upon permanence, and if death really is the end, then there is no value in anything. 'So I hated life' (17) . . . 'I hated all my toil' (18). Here is the sad echo of the Fall: '. . . you shall surely die' (Gen. 2:17). '. . . in the sweat of your face you shall eat bread, till you return to the ground . . .' (Gen. 3:19). Even the addictive restlessness of human labour is noted (23).

Yet such is the grace of God that the picture, though framed with blackness, has its inner brightness (24,25). Whatever pleasure, satisfaction and joy there is to be had in life and work comes from God's hand, and is to be enjoyed as such. Accepted as gifts of God and rightly used, food and drink and work are good in themselves (compare 1 Tim. 4:4). But if taken for the ultimate values in life, they fail us miserably.

Verse 26 is not a cynical expression of divine favouritism. Rather, its point is twofold: (*a*) that the best in life (wisdom, knowledge and joy) is for those who please God (compare Proverbs); (*b*) that the amassing of 'things' – the chosen obsession of sinners – is destined to frustration. Jesus' parable of the Rich Fool (Luke 12:15–21) is to the same point.

Turn verse 25 into a prayer of gratitude.

3:1–4:3 Time and eternity

Verses 1–9 form an evocative poem with no explicit 'moral', but several layers of probable meaning. The poem portrays the inexorable rhythms of life, which have their refreshing variety, and yet their repetitive futility (compare 1:4–11). It also reminds us that time is never 'neutral' or 'empty'; it always confronts us with a challenge or an opportunity. Time is always 'for' something. So the poem can be heard as a simultaneous call for patience (waiting for the right time) and for alertness (not to miss the time when it does come).

But our experience of time points beyond time (11). God has given us an inner 'intuition' of eternity, but one that is tantalising, for we cannot even know the whole of God's design. Like a man too close to a tapestry to see the whole pattern, but able to appreciate its smaller patterns, we can see enough to know that there *is* a design, and an eternal Designer (14). Furthermore, God is in complete control of the whole process of time and eternity. There will be no loose ends or carpet-corners (15). The appropriate response to such a God is to fear him (14b), as the author continued to do in the midst of his questioning and pessimism.

Meanwhile we should enjoy in life what is meant to be enjoyed (12, 13). To do otherwise is to reject *God's* gift. The sequence of thought in verses 11–13 suggests that even though we cannot see the total plan of God for *all* time, it is his gift and 'assignment' that we should find satisfaction in living and working in that segment of time he *has* given us.

But even as we do so, our enjoyment is spoiled by the sight of this morally topsy-turvy world. Verse 16 is expanded in 4:1–3 where the author reveals that he is no hardened cynic. He feels genuine grief and pain at the oppression and suffering of the world which is such that the unborn is happiest in his ignorance (3). However, if God rules time, then there will be time for judgement (3:17), and this in itself is a concealed hope, for Israelites knew that the righteousness by which God judged was also the righteousness by which he redeemed (see Isa. 45:21–25). But if you die before witnessing judgement on the wicked or vindication of the righteous – what then? Are you better off than the beasts? Verse 21 answers with a shrug. Only the Resurrection would remove the doubts for ever.

THOUGHT: What 'time' is it for you?

4:4–5:9 Faces in the crowd

The author has turned from his own experiments with life, to observation of others.

The workers (4:4–8). Even though he repeatedly asserts the value of hard work as a gift from God, he sees that sin has perverted that, too. The same selfish arrogance that plunged man into the Fall produces the drive to be better, bigger, richer . . . This competitive instinct (4) can contaminate not only secular labour, but even Christian work. It becomes obsessive, too, producing the sad loneliness of the 'workoholic' (8), for whom what God intended as a *means* (material resources to support oneself and one's family) has become a *goal*. The opposite, however, complacent laziness, is self-destructive folly (5, compare Prov. 6:6–11). Verses 6 and 9–12 present a balance: the peace of mind that comes from keeping a limit on one's expectations and demands (6), and the security that comes from close co-operation and companionship instead of either vicious envy or lonely, private enterprise (9–12).

The hero (13–16). Public heroes do not often grow old and stay heroes. The youthful leader who replaces the obstinate old king will some day be as unpopular as his predecessor. So much for popularity. Christians, as much as politicians, need to beware of putting their 'heroes' on pedestals. It is as spiritually dangerous for the 'hero' (compare Prov. 27:21) as for the 'worshippers'.

The worshipper (5:1–7). This is a warning to the worshipper who trips lightly to church, 'enjoys' all the talking, singing and devotions, is superficially moved to pious promises which he is unlikely to keep. God has not got a word in. Yet it is more important to hear and obey *him* than to offer *our* devotions (1, compare 1 Sam. 15:22. In Hebrew, to 'hear' also means to 'obey'). Note: 'the messenger' (6): probably the Temple messenger sent to collect payment of the vow so lightly made. On vows, compare Deuteronomy 23:21–23.

The officials (5:8,9). The oppression of the poor (how modern 8a sounds!) is a matter of grief (4:1), but not of surprise, once one understands the tendencies of bureaucracy. Two things are hinted at here: first, that the rights of the ordinary citizen can be denied simply by the endless confusion of 'red-tape' and the passing of responsibility from one official to another; second, that bureaucrats are vulnerable to the temptation to 'line their own pockets' by playing the system. Note: verse 9. It is difficult to decide if this verse is in favour of a king (RSV), or sees the king as just the top of the pyramid of exploitation (NIV). The context probably favours the second.

THOUGHT: Use 5:1,2 as a preparation for worship on Sundays.

5:10–6:12 'You can't take it with you'

Three proverbs about money (5:10–12) lead into a section mostly taken up with melancholy reflections on the fickleness of wealth, ending up with some unanswered questions (6:7–12).

Wealth is intrinsically unsatisfying. It never fulfils the desire it creates (10, compare 1 Tim. 6:9,10; Heb. 13:5). The more money there is, the more demands there will be on you (11), and if you go beyond the safe limits of personal consumption, expect indigestion at least (12, compare Ezek. 16:49 for a more pointed condemnation of the sins of 'surfeit').

Wealth is also disappointingly unreliable. The author produces a sickening 'see-saw' effect by stating, as a kind of pivot, his basic belief in work and wealth as God's gifts to be enjoyed (5:18–20), but then weighting on either side two examples of disaster and disillusionment (5:13–17 and 6:1–6). The first is a man who works desperately hard (17) to build up a heritage for his son, but loses the lot in some unfortunate business deal – a single false step (14). Not a crook, not a wastrel, yet he dies no better off than at his birth. The second is a man who goes through most of life with all the privileges it can offer, but ends up unable to enjoy it – perhaps through sickness, insanity, bankruptcy, loneliness. . . . What use then are all the blessings (long life and many children were prime Old Testament blessings)?

After such tragedies our instinct is to ask in bitterness, 'Why?' This author, facing up to the topsy-turvy absurdity of the world in its fallenness, and the finality of death in any case (6b), is more inclined to ask, 'Why not?' Moral choice in the present and expectation of the future are alike uncertain (6:12), not because there *can* be no certainty (God is still in control, compare 7:13,14, 8:12,13), but because of the state of this present world, and the limitations on our minds (10,11).

THOUGHT: What would you want to add, as a Christian, if faced with the pessimism of chapter 6?

7 'God made man upright, but . . .'

Verses 1–12: With a change of tactics, the author leaves the heap of depressing questions for a bombardment of proverbs which at first seem just as depressing. But its purpose is to make us look at the deeper realities – to face facts. The key-word is 'better'. What is 'better' is not usually what is easy or obvious. Funerals provide us with greater spur to serious reflection than birthdays (compare Ps. 90:12), or any other time of jollity (1,2, 4). Grief may produce a more realistic and sustained inner joy than superficial merriment (3, 6). The patience that completes things is better than the childish pride or anger that snuffs out enthusiasm for starting them (8). Nostalgia (10) is also unrealistic. It forgets the evil realities of earlier ages and provides a sentimental escape hatch from wrestling with the present. So be sensible (11,12).

Verses 13,14: Again the author shows his faith in God as sovereign. The inscrutable nature of things is part of God's purpose to lead us to a thinking trust. Verse 14b may sound cynical from this author, but, enlightened with God's revelation in Christ, it underlies the great affirmation of Romans 8:28.

Verse 15 is everyman's complaint. It was the fact that Job's friends in their dogmatic piety would not face. But what is our response to be? Verses 16–18 give an answer which goes further in pathetic, amoral cynicism than even this author usually goes. We should probably put these verses in quotation marks as one of the things included in verse 23a – 'all this I tested'. That it was not the author's own view is shown by the straight advice of 12:13. But it is certainly the almost universal attitude of our age.

None of his studying gets the author any nearer the ultimate truth he is looking for. Not even personal relationships give a reliable answer. The closest of them – the sexual – can be so depraved that they lead to a fate worse than death (26). Verse 28b must be regarded as the author's own unfortunate experience, not as a universal truth.

Verse 29 is a succinct summary of the doctrines of Creation and the Fall. Whatever may be the state of man and the world, it is neither God's fault nor God's original intention. We have created our own mess. But if we were upright once, may we not become so again? That is the tantalising question that lies beyond the horizon of this author. But at least it can be said that 'since futility was not the first word about our world, it no longer has to be the last.' (Kidner)

THOUGHT: Which 'day' is it for you (14)? Is your response as recommended?

8 The politics of public life

The art (and frustrations) of politics (1–9). There are obscurities in the Hebrew of these verses (as the different translations show), but they deal with the way a wise man acts within the constraints of political power ('the king'). Because of his insight (1), he will be called on to perform tasks which may be unwelcome or a burden to his conscience (3). Yet he is bound by his oath, which involves God (2), and bound by the superior power and authority of the king (3,4). In his dilemma he has to exploit both timing and procedures (5) to best advantage (compare 3:1–8), but no matter how skilfully he does so, there will be a lingering unpredictability about everything (7) – except death (8). Christians to whom God gives the wisdom appropriate to a calling to political involvement usually face the same dilemma: upholding standards of conscience, and yet having to cope with the realities of the fallen world and its power structures. 'Rendering to Caesar and . . . to God' is no *simple* choice.

Other public evils are observed in verses 10–14. The fickleness of human hero-worship was noted in 4:13–16. Its lack of moral discrimination or consistency is the point of verse 10, which either means that the wicked received praise in their lifetime even in the place where they carried out their unholy deeds, or that praise was lavished on them in death quite inappropriately in view of their evil lives. Verse 11 is an astute comment, that delayed justice is almost no justice, and certainly destroys the deterrent element in punishment. Perhaps, as well as being true in public life, it has something to say to the parent who habitually postpones discipline or chastisement – for yet another 'last chance'.

Verses 12–14 are a stark illustration of the tension between the author's faith and his observation. By faith he *knows* (12) of the ultimate security of the righteous who fear God, and of the perilous instability of the wicked (compare Pss. 1:4–6, 49:13–15; 73), yet he is offended when he sees the present *apparent* reversal of that expectation (14). Ironically, it was to be the fulfilment of verse 14a, in the wholly Righteous One who suffered what the wicked deserve, that would ultimately remove the charge of 'vanity'! (Note: GNB turns verse 12 into 'I know what they say . . .' and makes the author describe it as nonsense. But this is an unwarranted interpretation.)

So the chapter ends with characteristic bafflement, and a humble confession that the work of God in the world is beyond man's fathoming. The last sentence is a superbly deflating pin in the bubble of intellectual arrogance.

THOUGHT: Pray for Christians involved in politics or coping with structures of power in society, who face the dilemmas and compromises hinted at in verses 1–9.

9 'For tomorrow we die . . .'

Verse 1 is a combination of the faith of 8:12b with the inscrutability of 8:17. By faith we know we are in God's hands. By mere observation of the world we cannot tell whether God's attitude is acceptance or rejection ('love or hate'), for the criteria for making this judgement are rendered useless by death (2–6), by 'time and chance' (11,12), by human fickleness (13–18).

The 'sting' of death, which the author will not allow us to sentimentalise, is not only its finality, but its apparent neutralising of moral value in life (2) – which may account for the 'madness' of the living (3); its erasure of knowledge, incentive, emotion, and involvement; and the oblivion it brings (5,6). Yet even the sense of outrage ('this is an evil' 3) betrays an awareness that this cannot surely be the *last* word. For where did our awareness of morality and value come from if everything is as meaningless as this? 3:11 gave the answer.

Baffled as he is by death, the author does not allow it to poison life. Rather, it becomes a powerful spur to live life to its fullest, with hearty gratitude (10). Old Testament creation faith *affirmed* the goodness of the material and human blessings of this life – bread, wine, clothing, oil, marriage, work. The approval of God upon them (7b) is borne out in the way he could and would use them as vehicles for expressing his relationship with his people, in metaphor and sacrament. We have a higher motive for hearty living than verse 10b (though it is not unworthy in itself to be inspired to hard work by the fact of death putting an end to opportunity, compare John 9:4; Eph. 5:16; Phil. 1:22). Our motive is the experience of risen life in Christ and our future hope (compare Col. 3:1–4, 17, 23), which removes the sting of death and the threat of 'vanity' (compare 1 Cor. 15:55–58, note: '*not* in vain'). But this spiritual reality ought not to lead us to despise the enjoyment of the created goods of life which this author cheerfully advocates. The cure to 'materialism' (in the bad sense) is not pious anti-materialism, but the trust and gratitude that bring the whole of life under the lordship of Christ (compare Matt. 6:25–34; Col. 2:16–23; 1 Tim. 4:1–5).

THOUGHT: Are the plans of Christians any less vulnerable to 'time and chance' if we base them on our own ability to be 'swift, wise, intelligent and skilful'?

10 Society out of joint

This chapter is probably a deliberate interlude before the main theme is brought to a conclusion in chapters 11, 12. It consists almost entirely of proverbs, selected and arranged to fit in with the general tenor of the book.

Verse 1 continues the thought of 9:17,18, that it takes only a little folly or sin to destroy the fruits of wisdom and patience. How much easier it is to create bad feeling by our words and actions than to work at the building up of relationships and understanding. 'Right' and 'left' (2) were common synonyms in ancient cultures for 'good', 'safe', 'wise', and 'evil', 'sinister', 'foolish', respectively. The way of folly was fully exposed in Proverbs. The points made here include: the fool's inability to conceal what he is (he might as well announce it, 3); the way that foolish talk tends to degenerate by its very volume, into dangerous wickedness (13) – which shows again that the folly concerned is moral and spiritual obtuseness, not simple silliness (compare Matt. 12:33–37).

Yet the state of the world is so absurd that we may well end up being governed by such fools (5–7), and if there is 'folly in high places', 'proceeding from the ruler', then no wonder society is out of joint. One might add that the author, angered as he is by social injustice (4:1, 5:8), does not regard a simple reversal of power roles as an advancement of justice, but as a piling of absurdity on top of injustice. It may be that it is the dangers of socio-political involvement that are in his mind (compare 4) as he relates the otherwise 'obvious' proverbs of verses 8–11. This work can be dangerous and laborious, and occasionally the only alternative to success proves to be fatal (11). The author's concern for practical politics and the integrity and maturity of government emerges again in verses 16,17. Such things may not be able to provide ultimate answers to the deeper questions of life and death (though some modern politicians seem to believe so), but they are nonetheless morally important.

THOUGHT: Christ provides a higher motive for guarding our secret thoughts and words than verse 20 (Matt. 5:44–48)!

11 and 12 Remember your Creator

In chapters 11 and 12, before he signs off (12:9–12), the author makes a great effort to be positive in his concluding advice, even though he does not ignore the lurking shadows of futility and death – shadows which he has been unable to dispel by the light of his own reason, or the revelation as yet received. He makes three suggestions.

Live actively (11:1–6). It would be natural enough, given the perverse absurdity of life and the mockery of death, to sink into the apathy of despair and paralysed pessimism. When 'natural' man faces facts honestly he often does just that. But one thing has kept this author from that course. Not a refusal to face facts – he has exposed them more ruthlessly than is comfortable. Rather, he is sustained by his faith – his knowledge of God, the Creator, whose world this is, who is at work within it, however mysteriously (5). Now if God is thus involved in everything, even in a hidden way, then life is to be lived to the full – actively, boldly, and adventurously. Verse 1 is a trading metaphor, which commends enterprise and investment, but perhaps here also includes material generosity (which in the New Testament was regarded as a spiritual investment, compare 2 Cor. 9:6–14; Gal. 6:6–10). Life is full of stubborn realities beyond our control (like the weather, or the position of a fallen tree, verse 3). But such factors are to be wrestled with, turned into opportunities. There are uncertainties too (compare 9:11); all the more reason to redouble one's efforts (6), and ensure success. There is a right kind of Christian opportunism and pragmatism too – provided it is based on faith in the overall controlling and prospering will of God (see Isa. 55:10,11; Luke 12:35–48; 1 Cor. 3:5–15; Eph. 5:16; 2 Tim. 4:2).

Live heartily (11:7–10). The notes of enjoyment in life that have been sounded before, are struck again here. Life is good – while it lasts (8). Enjoyment of it is therefore no sin, but a positive duty (10a), especially in those years when the capacity for enjoyment is greatest – in youth (however *that* may be defined!). But youth itself is what this author would call a means – a 'time' of opportunity, not an end in itself. To make a cult of youth, to idolise it, is to turn it into 'vanity' (10b). But we are to live it with enjoyment and heartiness and also with responsibility. Verse 9b is not meant to be a sour spoil-sport. 'Judgement' does not mean God condemns the enjoyment just advocated. Rather it points out that only life lived consciously before God will be truly happy. This note of hearty joy in life and work, under God, reappears in the New Testament (Phil. 4:4–8; Col. 3:17, 23; 1 Thess. 5:16–19).

Live responsibly (12:1–8, 13,14). 'Remember' (1) meant much more to an Israelite than mere mental recollection. It meant an act of commitment and obedience (compare the emphasis on remembering in Deut. 4–11). To remember God as Creator is at once to admit with humility our own finitude before the sheer scale of God's work (compare 3:11; 8:17), our own perversity in spoiling what he created perfect (7:29), but also to grasp with faith the hidden fact of his ultimate control (7:13,14; 11:5). Such thoughts should fill our minds early enough to shape the course of life while we have the energy and potential to do so – that is, in youth, not in advanced old age. Verses 2–7 are a most beautifully moving and evocative poem of the last lap of life – with its weakness, loss of abilities and appetites, and gradual wearing out. The 'dust' of verse 7a re-echoes the curse of the Fall (Gen. 3:19b).

So, after a personal, but still anonymous, 'signature' (9–12), the author gives his final verdict on life (13), which shows him to be standing on the same rock as the rest of the Wisdom writers – the 'fear of God', expressed in obedience to his moral will. He still cannot see clearly beyond the 'vanity' that is death (8), yet remains convinced of the finality, totality and ultimate justice of God's judgement (14). Had he been able to see that justice at work on the Cross and in the Resurrection, he would have joined Paul in the triumph song of 1 Corinthians 15:55–58. 'Not in vain . . . in the Lord!'

THOUGHT: Fear God and keep his commandments; for this is the whole duty of man'.

Questions for further study and discussion on Ecclesiastes

1. Having worked through the book, do you agree with the interpretation of it offered in the Introduction and first section? Summarise how you would explain the meaning of the book.

2. Discuss your life goals. What are you really seeking after in all the things you do?

3. How do you react to the repeated advice to 'eat and drink and enjoy life'? Is it sub-Christian hedonism, or a valid corrective to pious asceticism? What does the example of Christ contribute?

4. What is wrong with Christian activism (see notes on chs. 2 and 4)? How can we avoid being too busy? How can we know when we are too busy?

5. People who are bereaved suffer added bitterness when friends leave them alone. Discuss how you can best help and comfort them. If you have been bereaved in what ways have you needed or discovered the strength that God and friends give?

6. Make a list of other paradoxes, along the lines of 7:1–8, drawn from your own experience of what is, unexpectedly, 'better'.

7. Reflecting on 8:1–9, identify some current political issues in which Christians involved in public life have to cope with conflict between principles and circumstances.

8. 'A right kind of Christian opportunism and pragmatism' (note on 11:1–6). Can you supply any practical examples of this? Compare some of the parables of Jesus that commend prompt, intelligent action.

Song of Solomon: Introduction

The Hebrew title is *The Song of Songs* – that is, the best, 'the most beautiful of songs' (GNB). The attribution to Solomon in 1:1 may indicate authorship, but the Hebrew could mean 'dedicated to' or 'about' Solomon, so authorship is uncertain. It is a series of love songs between a man and a woman. Since Hebrew has separate masculine and feminine forms of the 2nd personal pronoun 'you', it is usually possible to tell who is speaking to whom. Headings are helpfully given to the speeches in NEB, GNB, and NIV. Occasionally a group of friends speak, as a kind of chorus.

Analysis of the songs is difficult, since there are no explicit clues in the text of any life-setting. Some have taken it as a drama, with either two characters: Solomon and the Shulammite girl; or three characters: Solomon, the Shulammite, and her shepherd lover, who successfully holds the affection of the girl against the allurements of Solomon. Others see it as a cycle of wedding songs (compare NEB – 'bride', 'bridegroom' and 'companions'). It is perhaps best to take it as a collection of love lyrics. If there once was a connecting narrative or drama, for example, an oral folk-story, we have lost it. But the beauty of the poetry and the delight of its theme are not impaired thereby.

Interpretation of the book is equally varied, but there have been two main ways of handling it.

(*a*) *Allegorical*. The book owes its inclusion in the Canon of the Old Testament to the fact that Jewish Rabbis treated it as an allegorical description of the love relationship between God and his people. Many Christian interpreters followed suit and pressed every detail into some spiritual significance related to Christ and his Bride, the Church.

(*b*) *Literal*. The Song was written about the passion of human sexual love and it is full of evocative sexual symbolism which presents physical love and its accompanying emotions as things of intense delight, beauty and power. If we find such explicitness embarrassing, this may be simply our cultural reticence. But it may, more seriously, indicate an unbiblical view of sexuality itself as something embarrassing and slightly 'dirty'. We must remember that *God* created human sexuality as part of that 'image of God' that man was to be (Gen. 1:27). The delight of sexual complementarity and its physical expression are God's provision (Gen. 2:18–25).

Human love in all its forms (sexual, parent-child, brother, friend) derives from and reflects God's love, and can be used figuratively to describe God's relationship with his people (compare Hosea's use of marriage imagery). It is therefore legitimate to allow the Song to lead us, at a secondary level, to reflect on the richness of our relationship to God in Christ, so long as we remember that the *primary* purpose is to rejoice in human love for its own good sake.

Song of Solomon: Analysis

No division of the Song can be dogmatically asserted in the absence of any clear knowledge of the story or drama behind it. The following, based on the Good News Bible, is a convenient division for our study.

1:1–2:7	**A dialogue of love**
2:8–3:5	**Day of love: Night of dreams**
3:6–5:1	**Solomon's procession: The Shulammite's faithfulness**
5:2–6:3	**A night search rewarded**
6:4–8:4	**Love's mutual admiration**
8:5–14	**Love triumphant**

1:1–2:7 The First Song

The divison into six songs here adopted follows that of the GNB, but it is by no means a clear-cut division. This first song, ending at the appeal to the 'daughters of Jerusalem' (2:7, compare 3:5, 8:4), contains the opening declarations of love. The first speaker (2–4a) is a girl who has apparently been brought to the palace by the king. She is praised by friends (courtiers, the harem?) in verse 4b, but is embarrassed by her tanned skin (5, Kedar, a Bedouin tribe, whose tents are of black goat hair). This is due to her country origin and life (6). She has been guarding the vineyard in the sun and unable to look after her own 'vineyard' – her complexion (white skin was a mark of beauty in women). Verse 7 is addressed to her lover, whom some take to be a shepherd she has had to leave behind, but the oscillation between kingly and pastoral qualities in the male lover is confusing. Verse 8 is his reply, which he follows with some complimentary remarks (9–11). 'Horses', 9b, were highly prized and expensively ornamented, so the comparison was flattering!

Verses 12–14 are from the woman. 'Nard', or spikenard, was an expensive aromatic perfume, used as a symbol of love upon Jesus at Bethany (Mark 14:3). A sachet of crushed myrrh placed in the bosom also gave forth a strong fragrance, while henna from Engedi (an oasis near the Dead Sea) was both cosmetic and aromatic. The woman thus compares her lover with all that to her would be pleasing, potent, and highly valued. Verse 15 – the man; verse 16a – the woman; verses 16b–17, both together, suggesting a pastoral setting for their love. Some see these verses as the woman's longing for her country shepherd-lover, while 'imprisoned' in the palace. The country imagery continues: 2:1 – the woman ('rose': an unidentifiable wild flower); verse 2 – the man, with an 'evergreen' compliment! Verses 3–7 – the woman recalls a 'feast' of love. Verse 4 is an example of originally erotic symbolism that has been used spiritually of God's protective, providing love, and enshrined in a Christian song to that effect.

Verse 7, repeated like a refrain at 3:5 and 8:4, is slightly ambiguous. It may mean, 'do not arouse the passions of love prematurely or artificially' (as might have happened within the harem). Thus RSV and NIV. Or it may be a plea not to disturb one or both of the lovers (see NEB, GNB).

2:8–3:5 The Second Song

A day of love (2:8–17). This song is spoken almost entirely by the woman. The first half describes a delightful day in the countryside. The lover arrives (8,9), with his irresistible invitation (10). The description of him conveys youthful vigour and athleticism. The season, appropriately, is spring, the universal season for young love. Verses 11–13 are exquisitely beautiful in their evocation of the sights, sounds and scents of spring in Palestine. In verse 14 the man compares his beloved to a dove, and asks her to sing to him. Verse 15, which is otherwise inexplicable, is probably her song – a snatch of a vineyard song, since she had been a vineyard keeper (1:6). It probably also implies a hope that nothing will spoil the 'vineyard' of their loving relationship. Verse 16a – another expression of love that easily lends itself to spiritual application. Verse 17 is a farewell and an arrangement to meet again – either later that night, or the next morning. It is unclear whether 17a means the daybreak or the coming of night, but the former is more probable.

A night of dreams (3:1–5). After such a day, the woman's heart is filled with longing. These verses may describe actual disappointment and search – if, perhaps, 2:17a is an arrangement for her lover to come that night and he had broken it. Or, more probably, the verses may be all a dream.

'By night' (1) may mean 'that night', or perhaps 'night after night' (NEB, GNB), as she repeatedly pines for her lover. Those who regard her as in love with a shepherd while kept in Solomon's harem, see this as her longing dream to be free and reunited with her true love.

3:6–5:1 The Third Song

Solomon's procession (3:6–11). Solomon travels in regal splendour! The 'column of smoke' was not only the dust, but the fragrance of censers and perfumes. No natural country smells for the king! Surrounded by armed escorts (7b, 8), Solomon is carried in a magnificent portable throne, regal even to the crown on his head. It is not stated where he is going, nor who is speaking these words. But it is probably a procession to the northern home of the Shulammite woman, designed to woo her. The words are perhaps spoken by some highly impressed local inhabitants.

Chapter 4:1–15 is the poetry of admiring love. Whether or not it is all from the same male speaker – Solomon – is uncertain. It may be that verse 6a, which echoes the words of the tryst in 2:17, is an interruption and that after this, either in reality, or in the thoughts of the Shulammite, the shepherd-lover 'out-woos' Solomon (7–15). The comparisons of verses 1–5 may not strike us as epitomes of tact, but the point in each case is not the whole but some feature of the object of comparison. Thus 'a flock of goats' (1) – black and flowing; 'shorn ewes' with twins (2) – smooth, white and regular; 'pomegranate' (3) – soft and russet coloured; 'tower' (4) – well-shaped ('built for an arsenal' is a guess at an unknown Hebrew phrase), and obviously decorated with necklaces; 'twin fawns' (5) – equal, soft and fresh.

Verse 7 reminds many interpreters of the Bride of Christ who he will one day be able to address in such terms (compare Eph. 5:26,27; Jude 24).

Amana (8) is the range of which Senir, or Hermon, is the highest peak (9,000 ft), on the northern border of Israel with Lebanon.

The imagery of a locked garden (12) which is used of the woman (who is now being addressed as 'bride'), is undoubtedly intended to portray an exclusive love. The Shulammite will be one man's wife only. Her beauty, attractiveness and refreshment (13–15) are locked, until she chooses to open them to her chosen one (16). *If* the earlier verses have contained something of a wooing contest, then the winner, presumably the shepherd, is overwhelmed with the joy of 'entering the garden' (5:1a) of his bride's love. The good wishes of their friends (5:1b) draw a curtain over their nuptial delights.

5:2–6:3 The Fourth Song

A night search (5:2–8). Again, it is uncertain whether this vivid scene is reality or a dream. It has dream-like qualities of missed opportunity, frustration, and a nightmarish violence. The lover arrives late at night (the heavy dew, 2b), and is met with what, in the light of verses 4,5, is probably playful teasing (3). His mysterious disappearance is typical of disturbed dreams. After her fruitless searching and rough handling, the Shulammite cries out to the women of Jerusalem for help.

The questions of 5:9 and 6:1 may be entirely 'face-value', or they may be the rather sarcastic remarks of the ladies of the harem, irritated by the Shulammite's loyalty to her shepherd lover. Either way, the first question inspires a description of her lover (5:10–16) which is clearly a counter-balance to the compliments that were flowing in her own direction in chapter 4. 'Gold' (11) denoted nobility, not colour; his hair was as black as her own (11b). The point of verse 12 probably lies in the rapid movement of birds drinking water, coupled with the purity of the 'whites' of his eyes. Verse 13; spicy 'after-shave' is clearly nothing new (though it was probably the lover's *beard* that was perfumed)! Verses 14,15 denote the perfect craftsmanship in the lines of his muscular body. 'Altogether desirable' (16) – indeed! But whether it would help the 'daughters of Jerusalem' in their search was another matter! In any case, the lover had already gone (6:2,3). The reference is to his shepherd's pastures and garden back home. Verse 3, compare 2:16, 7:10. If chapter 5 was a dream, by 6:2 we are back in reality. The woman knows where her lover really is; it was only in the nightmare that she lost him. Their love is a mutual possession (3a) not to be destroyed.

6:4–8:4 The Fifth Song

The male lover embarks on another outpouring of praise. The language is similar to 4:1–5, and the speaker is the same as there. Some take it to be Solomon making a renewed bid for the Shulammite's affection. 'Tirzah' (4) – a beautiful city that was capital of the northern kingdom of Israel for some time. 'Terrible as an army with banners' (4b, 10b): the phrase is obscure, but appears to denote awe-inspiring, majestic presence. So outstanding is this girl that she outshines the rest of the harem (8,9) who, grudgingly or otherwise, have to admit her excellence (9b, verse 10 may be their comments, as in RSV, or it may be attached to verse 11, as in GNB).

At this point, the 'story-line', if there was one, is lost and we are in confusion. Verses 11,12 may be Solomon describing how he first set eyes on the Shulammite, accidentally, and was overwhelmed at first sight (12, compare NEB, GNB). Or they may be spoken by the Shulammite, perhaps describing how she was 'captured' by Solomon, or his 'talent scouts', while innocently working on the farm. Likewise, verse 13 is open to several interpretations. It may be the cry of her local friends as she is carried off (13a), answered by the Shulammite's own unawareness of her beauty (13b). Or it may be that verse 13a is the call of the ladies of the harem as the Shulammite goes back to her own people, answered, in verse 13b, by her refusal to be a dancing entertainer. 'A dance before two armies': probably the name of a folk dance involving two rows of dancers.

The poetic admiration of the woman continues in chapter 7. This may be Solomon again, or it may be the harem (compare 13a) preparing her for the king (compare 5b, unless the reference there to the king is purely metaphorical). 'Tower of Lebanon' (4), probably the reference is to straightness rather than prominence.

In verse 9b, RSV margin is preferable. The woman interrupts the flow of praise, saying – 'Then let my kisses flow, like wine, to my lover' (as NIV, GNB). If Solomon was the speaker up to this point, this may be her final denial of him in preference for her true love (10). Or it may just be part of the intimate dialogue of love, if verses 6–9a have been spoken by her bridegroom. Verses 10–13 re-echo the pastoral setting of 2:12, 13, and the season is still spring, with its blossoming beauty. 'Mandrakes' (13, as well as being fragrant, were prized as aphrodisiacs (compare Gen. 30:14–16).

Such is the bride's longing to express her love and receive his (3, compare 2:6) that she is impatient with conventions that confined any public demonstration of affection to close relatives (8:1,2).

8:5–14 The Sixth Song

The concluding song celebrates the final uniting of the lovers in marriage. In verse 5a it is perhaps the villagers who see the Shulammite and her lover approaching. He points out the place where he first made known his love for her (5b). A seal (6) symbolised precious ownership – both in emotion ('heart') and in fact ('arm' as public protector). If there has been a contest for the love of the Shulammite, then 6b and 7 are a comment on the endurance of true love, and its pricelessness.

Verses 8–10 are puzzling, but are usually taken to refer to the guarding of chastity. The brothers of verses 8, 9, in view of their older sister's experience, prepare for the day when their young sister reaches the age of courtship. If she guards her own chastity ('is a wall') they will adorn her. But if she is in danger of being too easily won ('is a door'), they will guard her chastity themselves. Verse 10 is the Shulammite's comment. She had stood firm in her chastity – meaning either that she had resisted the allurement of Solomon and preserved herself for her true bridegroom, or simply (if the 'Solomon versus the Shepherd' theory is mistaken), that she had been faithful and pure in the days of her pre-marital betrothal. To her bridegroom, therefore, she brought a 'wholeness' ('peace', 10b) of contentment in an undefiled love.

Verses 11,12 amplify the comment in verse 7b that love cannot be bought – indeed to try to do so is contemptible. The bride thinks of the wealthy vineyard of Solomon which he hired out to tenant cultivators. But she has her own 'vineyard' – herself (compare 1:6 where it was her beautiful complexion), which she has jealously kept and not hired out. Solomon is welcome to his rent, and the farmers to their profit (12b); she is content to give herself wholly to her bridegroom. This may be her parting shot at Solomon after his failure to win her, or (again, if there is no implied 'Solomon versus Shepherd' contest), simply an act of imagination in which she says she would despise even King Solomon if he tried to 'buy' her. The Song, for all its heady savouring of the delights of courtship and love, thus remains true to the Old Testament ideal of pre-marital chastity, monogamy and marital faithfulness. Such principles do not cramp or dull, but rather enhance and strengthen the ecstasies of human sexual love – God's beautiful gift to be enjoyed in God's way.

Questions for further study and discussion on Song of Solomon

1. Has this book enriched your appreciation of human sexuality and love? Do you agree that this is its primary purpose?

2. Some people try to turn sexual love into something nasty and cheap. How can Christians resist this in themselves and in society?

3. What particular elements or verses in the Song inspire comparison with Christ's love and our relationship to him?

4. How can the Song be used in Christian worship?

5. What are the special blessings and difficulties facing those to whom God has given 'the gift of being single'?

6. In what ways has your reading of the Song of Solomon led you closer to God?

7. In what ways might a couple preparing for marriage benefit from a reading of the Song of Solomon?

8. Especially in some parts of the western world we find it difficult to express love in words. What can we learn from the Song of Solomon about this?

Isaiah 1–39: Introduction

Isaiah of Jerusalem stands as the greatest of the 'classical' prophets of the eighth century BC. Amos and Hosea prophesied in Northern Israel in the previous generation (Isaiah shows indebtedness to both), and Micah was his contemporary in Judah. The eighth century was a time of considerable wealth and power in both Israel and Judah, but the prophets saw the gross inequalities, oppression and injustices. They refused to be silent about this for they saw it as a denial of the spiritual demands of the covenant relationship with God.

Isaiah had a long ministry, from about 736 BC to at least 701 BC – the latter being the date of the great Assyrian crisis and Sennacherib's siege of Jerusalem, to which the climactic last chapters of this part of the book relate. Jewish tradition has it that Isaiah continued until he was put to death by the evil king Manasseh in the next century.

He seems to have been an official Temple prophet, with direct access to the monarch, closely associated with the court and politico-religious hierarchy. Their arrogance and pomp created in Isaiah a characteristic loathing of all things 'high and mighty' – except for God himself, whose awesome, exalted holiness was an axiom of his thinking ever since his call-vision.

His prophecies are not arranged in strict chronological order, but rather grouped into fairly clear sections, as seen in the analysis of contents.

Isaiah: Analysis

1:1–20	The opening summons
1:21–5:30	Accusations against Jerusalem and Judah
6:1–13	The Prophet's call and commission
7:1–12:6	Prophecies of judgement and hope from the period of the first Assyrian crisis, about 733
13:1–23:18	Prophecies concerning other nations
24:1–27:13	'The apocalypse of Isaiah': Visions of final judgement and salvation
28:1–31:19	The Assyrian threat: God's help or human alliance?
32:1–35:10	Further visions of the New Age
36:1–39:8	The later Assyrian crisis, about 701 BC: The testing of Hezekiah

1:1–20 God's summons

This great opening prophecy almost certainly speaks in warning of the near total destruction (7–9) evident in the aftermath of Sennacherib's invasion, 701 BC. It may have been placed here at the beginning because it is so powerfully representative of the themes of Isaiah's preaching.

God's accusation (2,3) begins with a summons to the universe to witness the court trial about to begin (compare Deut. 30:19; 32:1; Ps. 50:4). God, who is both judge and plaintiff, introduces himself as Father (2b). Sonship requires gratitude, trusting dependence and obedience (compare Mal. 1:6). Israel, in their rebellion, have failed in all of these. Even domestic animals display these qualities towards their owners ('know' – a very rich word, denotes these aspects of practical relationship), but Israel fails even to recognise that she has fallen below the beasts. Moral disobedience and mental and spiritual obtuseness go together (compare Hos. 4:1–6).

Isaiah's expansion (4–7) of the direct words of God adds some colour to the word 'rebelled' (2). This is sharpened by the title given to God – the 'Holy One of Israel'. Then Isaiah proceeds to an illustration (5, 6): they are like a slave who is repeatedly disobedient, repeatedly beaten, until there is nowhere left to beat! But still he comes back for more! Such was the state of Judah after Sennacherib's invasion (7,8). Sennacherib's own catalogue of destruction and captives confirms this. And Jerusalem, though miraculously spared, is like a tottering shack on a derelict allotment (8)! Verse 9 combines the fact of God's grace for a remnant (a theme to be developed later, see 10:20–23) with a breath-taking comparison of Jerusalem with Sodom and Gomorrah – bywords for total and *deserved* destruction. One can imagine the angry reaction of the people – especially the Temple officials (it is quite likely that this prophecy was delivered in the Temple, see 11–14). Undaunted, Isaiah repeats the insult – making it even more personal (10).

God's explanation (11–17) is no less shocking. He is tired of the whole round of ritual observance, sacrifices, offerings, festivals, assemblies, prayers, because they have been divorced from obedience to the demands of the covenant. The blood on their hands (15b) was not just that of animals, but of the victims of injustice and oppression. Will the people change? Verses 16,17 summarise major appeals that will be developed later.

God's offer (18–20) is a final attempt to bring the people to their senses. It is a conditional pardon – conditional upon true repentance shown by obedience (16,17 and 20) – but a pardon that is complete (scarlet and crimson were the deepest and fastest dyes of the ancient world).

THOUGHT: The power of God's forgiveness is sufficient for the deepest human guilt.

1:21–31 Righteousness: human and divine

This word of judgement begins as a funeral lament (compare Lam. 1:1) over Jerusalem. Three pictures are used to show up her corrupt state: a once faithful wife, now turned to prostitution (compare Hos. 5:4; Jer. 3:8); pure silver that has unnaturally returned to its unrefined dross; good wine that has been adulterated. The cause of the decline is traced to corrupt political and judicial leadership. Those responsible for the elimination of injustice were in league with it ('companions of thieves')! Those without the natural protection of family and land (orphans and widows) and unable to bribe, were neglected.

So, upon this perversion of human justice, the divine justice will be vented (24–26). Verse 24, with its majestic names of God, was the sort of oracle often heard against foreign nations. Here it is startlingly and ominously turned on Israel. God's enemies are within his own people! But, by returning to the metaphor of verse 22a, God shows that his action will be not solely punitive, but purgative (25). His purpose is to purify and restore, until Jerusalem once more has integrity and justice in her social life and is thus faithful again to the demands of the covenant (26). An implication of this passage is that righteousness is a gift of God which we are called on to maintain.

Verses 27,28, which may have been added later to the original self-contained oracle (21–26), summarise its point: God's judgement is a tool of his redemptive purpose, for it will distinguish the repentant from the rebels. We might wonder whether the 'justice' and 'righteousness' by which Zion will be redeemed belong to God or the people. The answer is probably both, but God's justice is certainly prior. For the righteousness of God is demonstrated both in judgement and redemption (compare Isa. 45:21), the cross being the supreme and central focus of both, so that Paul can declare that the 'righteousness of God is revealed in the gospel' (Rom. 1:16,17). But the mark of repentance and the response to redemption are to live according to the righteous will of God, 'to do good and seek justice' (compare 1:17).

Verse 29 may refer to idolatry and fertility rites, or simply to arrogant trusting in one's own strength (of which the oak was a symbol). Those who exalt themselves will be destroyed by the 'spark' of their own deeds (31).

THOUGHT: Compare this 'lament' with Revelation 2:4,5 and reflect on the state of your own life and that of your local Christian community.

2:1–5 City of God

The fresh heading (1) probably stood at the head of a collection of Isaiah's early prophecies. The immediate context goes from 2:2–4:6 (prophecies of doom sandwiched between two visions of salvation after judgement), but the collection introduced at 2:1 may well extend further. 'The *word* which . . . he *saw*': the prophetic 'audio-visual' experience.

Verses 2–5 are a magnificent vision (also used by Micah, 4:1–5) of the state of mankind under God's rule at the consummation of history. Four points are made. (*a*) There will be a transformation of the world such that Mount Zion (a comparatively small hill) will be the highest mountain on earth (2). The language is geographical but the point is spiritual: mankind will see that what Zion stood for (the dwelling-place of God, the worship of God, the word of God) is the true centre and pinnacle of human life. (*b*) The response will be a wholehearted seeking of God and living in his way. The nations will flock to Zion for that is where the Lord's direction ('law') will be found (3). Where the Lord is acknowledged, his will is obeyed. The prophet here expresses Israel's awareness that their election and privilege (symbolised in the choice of Jerusalem) was not for them alone, but for the rest of mankind. This was explicit in the call of Abraham (Gen. 12:3) and enshrined in Psalms (for example, 22:27; 87) and prayer (1 Kings 8:41–43). This prophesied 'coming to' Jerusalem is not in conflict with the historical mission of the church setting out *from* Jerusalem to the ends of the earth (Luke 24:47; Acts 1:8). The purpose of that mission is indeed the 'ingathering' of the nations to true worship and obedience of God, focused now, not on a place, but a *person*, Jesus Christ (compare John 4:21–26; Heb. 12:22–24; 13:13–15). (*c*) There will be universal peace – not the outcome of man's efforts, but the gift of God, whose rule will be uncontested and unresisted. In response, mankind will replace warfare with a return to their original mandate – to use and enjoy creation as God intended (4). The combination of righteousness and peace is beautifully echoed in Psalm 85:10. (*d*) The prophecy finishes with a challenge (5). It is not a *dream* of what *might* be, which leads to despair or escapism, but a *vision* of what *will* be, which leads to repentance (vs. 6, 9) and obedience (5), which exposes sin and guides into the future.

THOUGHT: the Christian sees in this prophecy a hope that 'looks beyond all the conflicts of the present time towards the moment when God will bring to completion the work of new creation which he began on Easter morning. In this respect, the Christian church . . . can see itself as addressed in the last verse' (that is, v. 5) (Kaiser).

2:6–22 The Day of the Lord

Since this passage is addressed to God, and since Isaiah was probably an official Temple prophet, it may be that this prophecy arose in the Temple when he was expected to pray for the forgiveness of the people (compare 9b) and for the 'Day of the Lord' which, it was thought, would bring the fullness of God's salvation and blessing. But, overwhelmed by the sin of the people (compare 6:5), he is unable to pray thus, and instead breaks into this declaration of rejection and fearful judgement.

Verses 6–11 set the themes which are then developed and repeated throughout the rest of the chapter, and recur later (for example, 3:16; 5:15). The material prosperity of the nation (7, a reference which dates this prophecy early, before the Assyrian war) is contrasted with its spiritual and moral rottenness. There is superstition (6b), foreign alliances (6c), weaponry that was unneeded and prohibited (7b, compare Deut. 17:16), idolatry (8) and arrogance (11). It is the arrogance which so provokes the Lord's anger, for it reckons that security is found in such things. But when the Lord acts in judgement even the caves will be no security. The desperate picture of verse 10 comes back like a refrain at verses 19 and 21 and remained a figure of the terror of judgement (see Rev. 6:15,16).

The horrid irony is that though in their arrogance they will not submit to the Lord, their Creator and Redeemer, yet they 'bow down to the work of their own hands' (8). The only humility they know is before the gods of their own creation – in their day, wealth, secure defences, political power, speculators about the future (6), in ours, much the same, plus the worship of science, progress, technology. . . . But when man *himself* is brought low (17), then the idols will become irrelevant (18) encumbrances (20).

The 'Day of the Lord', in popular expectation, was to be another of God's great saving acts, the completion of the earlier great 'days' of the Exodus, the Conquest, the choice of Jerusalem. Amos had reversed that hope with his shattering prediction of judgement (Amos 5:18–20). Isaiah, with his pointed repetition of 'that day', stands in the same tradition.

THOUGHT: The final verse (22) destroys for ever any illusion we might have that we can build the world of verses 2–4.

3:1–4:1 The price of prosperity

As a member of the court scene, Isaiah knew the ruling establishment and its ways thoroughly, and this chapter of judgement is directed at them.

Verses 1–11 were perhaps addressed to a gathering of such leading men. Against the background of the prosperity of Judah during Isaiah's ministry, the doom announced must have been shocking indeed. Isaiah predicts the effects of siege and collapse – famine (1), loss (through deportation) of military, political and spiritual leadership (2, 3), anarchy (4) and the social chaos it produces (5–7). Since the destruction of Jerusalem is also hinted at (6b), the fulfilment of these verses must be seen in the Babylonian conquest, not the Assyrian invasion of Isaiah's own later lifetime. The grounds of the judgement are given in verses 8,9 – and again it is the arrogant disregard for the Lord that is uppermost. The sin of the upper classes is blatant and shameless. Their oppressive practices, greed, injustice and other evils (to be specified in chapter 5), have become so socially acceptable that they are scarcely thought of as sin. Therefore no trouble is taken to conceal them (9a). The same is still true today. Wealth and power have a way of cushioning the conscience. Being compared to Sodom (compare 1:9, 10) is a powerful way of re-awakening it.

Verses 12–15 address a wider audience ('my people'), perhaps at a great festival gathering in Jerusalem, and speak of the rulers in the third person. But the theme is the same: the people face destruction because of the evil abuse of power by the aristocracy ('elders and princes' 14). Their duty is to care for the Lord's 'vineyard' (his people and land) as stewards, in the spirit of Psalms 72 and 101, but they treat it as enemy spoil.

In verses 16–4:1 Isaiah sees that arrogance and oppression by the powerful is not a masculine preserve. It is not the cosmetics and finery in themselves that he condemns, but what underlies them. He can see as clearly as Amos before him (Amos 4:1–3) that the luxuries and lewdness of these women are paid for by the exploitation of the poor. Therefore they, too, will suffer horribly in the coming destruction – as they did; female captives were often barbarously treated. Those left widowed, unmarried or childless will forego even the rights of a concubine slave (4:1, compare Exod. 21:10) in order to be owned by any man left alive.

THOUGHT: Could it be that some of *our* luxuries are paid for by injustices conveniently distant from our immediate vision?

4:2–5:7 The branch and the vineyard

4:2–6: Rounding off this collection of prophecies is a return to the same note as 2:2–4 – salvation after judgement. As bluebells spring up among the ashes of a bracken fire, so new life will come to God's people after the purging fires of judgement (4b). The picture is not just of a rebuilding of the old, but a new growth which will far surpass the former beauty and glory (2). 'Branch' (2), literally 'new shoot', in this context refers to the fresh work of God and its 'fruit', not the Messiah (though it is used elsewhere as a messianic figure: Isa. 11:1; Jer. 23:5, 33:15; Zech. 3:8, 6:12). The 'fruit' would be a harvest of righteousness (compare Ps. 85:10–13) among those who would be 'holy (3), and 'washed' (4) by the Lord's purging. The result would be a community fit for the Lord to dwell in once more – (in contrast to the defiance of his presence in 3:8). The pictures of cloud and fire symbolised his guidance, presence and protection (5,6, compare Exod. 13:21, 40:34–38). Note the combination of individual holiness and salvation in verse 3 ('recorded for life' – God's personal knowledge of the names of his own, compare Dan. 12:1; Luke 10:20; Rev. 13:8, 20:12–15) with the corporate 'assemblies' of verse 5.

5:1–7: We may imagine this brilliant and powerful parable being told at the great autumn harvest and vintage festival (the Feast of Tabernacles, Deut. 16:13–15) to the crowds of singing Judeans thronging Jerusalem (3). Isaiah begins with what appears at first to be just another vintage song. But he refers to a 'friend' and his vineyard. 'Vineyard' was a common metaphor for a bride (compare Song of Sol. 4:12–15, 8:12), so the story that follows has a double meaning. In spite of laborious and loving care, his friend's 'vineyard' has yielded bitter wild grapes (2). Then the 'friend' interposes with a question: was *he* in any way to blame? (4). What then was to be done? Unfaithfulness in a bride was a capital offence (Deut. 22:23,24). Unfruitfulness in a vineyard was reason enough to abandon it (5,6a). The 'friend' reveals his identity in 6b. Only *God* commands the rain. The point is made, but Isaiah hammers home the identifications (7a), and concludes with a superb word-play (7b): 'justice' (*mishpat*), 'bloodshed' (*mishpach*); 'righteousness' (*tsedaqah*), 'cry of pain' (*tse'aqah*).

THOUGHT: This is probably the most poetic and powerful example of a recurring theme in Scripture – the pain and disappointment God suffers through his people's frustration of his investment of labour and love in them. What 'return' is your life providing at present? Ponder verse 4.

5:8–30 (and **10:**1–4)
A catalogue of social evil

The catalogue of six 'woes' in this chapter, to which should probably be added 10:1–4 as the seventh of the original list, spells out in detail the social evils that Isaiah has condemned earlier. 'Woe to' combines a cry of 'shame' (NEB) with a note of imminent doom.

Against covetous land-hoarders (8–10). The land was God's inheritance-gift to Israel, but he retained ultimate ownership of it and had decreed the pattern of land-tenure (Lev. 25:23). Every family was to have a share in it (compare the allotments in Josh. 13–19), and land was to be maintained within the kinship patterns, not treated as a mere commercial asset. But the influx of wealth from trade and tribute since the time of Solomon's empire had created a wealthy elite who accumulated estates for themselves by dispossessing an impoverished peasantry (compare Mic. 2:2–5). Such disregard for the covenant will be punished by frustration of their greed.

Against debauched godlessness (11–17). The condemnation is not only on the social parasitism of the nobility (drunk in the morning, they could hardly work in the day), but of their spiritual blindness (12b). Verses 13, 14, compare Hosea 4:6, 11,12.

Against scoffers (18,19). Economic prosperity and apparent political security had bred contempt for the demands of God and the prophetic threat of judgement. The metaphor of verse 18 probably implies that judgement is inevitably 'attached' to sin. The taunt to God to act (19) was hurled at Christ (Matt. 27:40–43) and drew an answer from Peter (2 Pet. 3:3–15). It betrays a particularly hardened unbelief that makes the merciful forbearance of God all the more remarkable.

Against truth-twisters (20). Unbelief justifies itself by specious perversions of the moral order. Jesus exposed its fatal fruit in the Pharisees (Matt. 12:22–37); Paul describes its moral effects (Rom. 1:18–32).

Against arrogant intellectuals (21) – the close relatives of those who pervert God's truth. Here is the opposite to that true wisdom which is founded on fear of the Lord. Such people are even worse than fools (Prov. 26:12), for they are impervious to any correction.

Against corrupt judges (22,23), who are experts, but only in cocktails, not in delivering just verdicts (compare 1:17, and Prov. 31:4, 5).

Against oppressive legislators (10:1–4). This follows naturally. The wealthy and powerful provide themselves not only with perverted moral and intellectual justification, but also with a spurious legality, in defiance of covenant law (1,2).

Verses 24,25 pronounce the sentence; 26–30 summon the executioner – the fearful Assyrian military machine.

THOUGHT: 'There is no blessing upon ownership which is not morally justified. The Lord of man and of nature will make sure of that' (Kaiser, on verses 8–10).

6 Isaiah's call

This carefully dated account of Isaiah's call stands at the head of a section of his prophecies (6–12) which includes three great messianic oracles (chapters 7, 9, 11), interwoven with the certainty of imminent judgement. The death of Uzziah (around 736) marked the beginning of a decline in Judah's power, just as Assyrian ambitions rose. His death as a leper after an act of pride (2 Chron. 26:16–21) also symbolised Isaiah's message (compare 2:11–18).

The vision (1–4). Probably occurring within the Temple, Isaiah's vision of God is dominated by awesome majesty. 'Train' – his royal cloak, perhaps suggested by the clouds of incense. The 'seraphim' (compare Num. 21:6; Isa. 14:29, 30:6) were winged serpents with human features, representing the heavenly hosts of spiritual creatures who attend God. Though sinless, they shrink from seeing or being seen by God (2b), such is his overwhelming holiness. Their antiphonal song (3) combines the innermost perfection of God's nature ('holy'), his personal, redemptive name (LORD translates Yahweh), his power and resources ('of hosts'), and that visible, tangible revelation of his power which sustains and fills the earth ('glory').

The preparation (5–7). The sight, sound, shaking and smoke (compare Sinai, Exod. 19:16–19) fill Isaiah with fear as he identifies himself, in his sin and guilt, with his people. He cannot join in the praise but can merely confess his sin and await judgement (5). However, presumably at God's command, he is purified by the action of a seraph (6). The burning coal signified the efficacy of the altar as the place of atonement and forgiveness, applied to the place of conscious need. Isaiah, who would expose the sins of his people, knew himself to be but a forgiven sinner – the mark of all true servants of God.

The call (8–10). Thus cleansed and, to his surprise, still alive, Isaiah responds to God's call with a promptness which is in vivid contrast to Moses (Exod. 3,4) and Jeremiah (Jer. 1:6), but is comparable to Paul who had a similar sense of God's inexplicable mercy (1 Cor. 15:8–10). Verses 9,10 do not specify the content of his message, but its *effect*, expressed, in Hebraic fashion, as its intention. The tragic irony was that the word of God, in which lay the people's only hope of salvation, would become, by their rejection of it, the agent of their destruction. Precisely the same effect was foreseen by Jesus, the living Word, in Mark 4:11,12, quoting this passage.

The prospect (11–13). Isaiah was left in no doubt about the prognosis for his people, but the gleam of hope in the last line of verse 13 lies behind Isaiah's important 'Remnant' theology.

THOUGHT: *A spiritual equation:* recognition of God's holiness and glory + experience of God's forgiving grace = grateful obedience to God's call.

Questions for further study and discussion on Isaiah 1–6

1. Does 1:11–15 constitute a total rejection by God of the whole sacrificial and festival cult? Compare Jeremiah 7:21–23; Hosea 6:6; Amos 5:21–24; Micah 6:6–8 and Matthew 23. If not, what is its precise meaning?

2. The picture of 2:2,3 suggests that others will find God as they are drawn *to* the people of God. Do you find this an adequate picture of mission? How, if at all, is it modified in the New Testament?

3. If Isaiah were living now how would he phrase 1:17? Discuss and pray about any practical steps you or your group could take.

4. In what ways can the luxurious life-style of the West be said to be at the expense of justice elsewhere in the world (compare ch. 3)? What can be done about it?

5. Using a concordance, make a study of the themes of the new Zion in Scripture (compare 4:2–6) – culminating in Revelation 21.

6. What other examples are there in Scripture of the theme of 'divine investment' being disappointed by human failure (compare 5:1–7)?

7. Compare Isaiah's call with other calls in both the Old and New Testaments. Are there principles applicable to any call to Christian service?

8. Discuss how we may recapture or deepen our awareness of the holiness and greatness of God.

7 'Immanuel': promise or warning?

The political situation, (verse 1, compare 2 Kings 16 and 2 Chron. 28) in about 733 BC was that Israel (the northern kingdom) and Syria, in rebellion against Assyria, were trying to force Judah into alliance with them. King Ahaz planned to ally with Assyria against them – a course both politically and religiously disastrous. The meeting between Isaiah and the king seems to have taken place when these plans had been made, but not yet carried out. The presence of Isaiah's son (3) was itself a prophetic sign: his name signified both judgement ('*only* a remnant will return'), and hope ('but a remnant *shall* return'). That this is not explained probably means that Ahaz and Isaiah had met before. God's message to Ahaz (4–9) was simple: 'The conspiracy of your enemies will fail; trust me.' The command to ask for a sign was to test the king. Would he accept proof of Isaiah's prophecy – proof that would call imperatively for faith and the end of faithless political alliances? But Ahaz would not, for his mind was already made up, though he cloaks his unbelief with a pious quote of Scripture (12, compare Deut. 6:16).

The Immanuel sign (14–17) is deliberately ambiguous: it could be a promise or a warning. Its ultimate fulfilment in the birth of Jesus (Matt. 1:22, 23) tends to dominate our interpretation, but we must also see it in its context as a sign to Ahaz and Judah and therefore look for a meaning closer to the historical events. The word translated 'young woman' refers to a girl of marriageable age – normally but not necessarily a virgin. The immediate point of the sign lay not in the state of the mother or a miracle conception, but in the name and life of the child. It cannot have referred to a child of the king, for Hezekiah was already born, or of Isaiah, whose next son was differently named (8:3). A collective or general interpretation is probably best, that is, that within a period of months (conception to birth) the land will be delivered and in relieved gratitude mothers will name children 'Immanuel' – 'God with us' (for a similar naming in response to events, see 1 Sam. 4:21). Verse 14 thus corresponds to verse 16 in interpretation. However, within a few years (by the time such children reach moral discretion) the land will be reduced to 'starvation diet' ('curds and honey' – nomad's food) by war and destruction. Verse 15 thus corresponds to verse 17. The remainder of the chapter (18–25) amplifies the devastation to be suffered under Assyria – Assyria whom Ahaz imagined he was 'hiring' for help, but whom God was 'hiring' (20) as the tool of his judgement.

THOUGHT: Beware the temptation to use the Word of God to justify disobedience to the command of God. God's exasperation is understandable (13).

8 'The rock': refuge or ruin?

Verses 1–4: Another of Isaiah's sons is given a prophetic name; he will be a living proof of the truth of his father's prophecy. His name meant 'Spoil-speed-prey-hasten', and indeed the fulfilment of verse 4 took place within his childhood. The point of the writing, witnessing (1,2) and sealing up (1b) of these predictions was not only to make them public, but also to ensure that future generations would have no doubt that the name and prophecy had preceded the events.

Verses 5–10: Shiloah was a water conduit into Jerusalem, and Isaiah makes it a symbol of God's promised protection (compare Ps. 46:4,5). But since Ahaz, in calling on Assyria, has led the people to reject God's provision, they will be all but ('up to the neck') swept away in judgement. 'River' (7) is the Euphrates. In their desperation, the people will cry Immanuel's name as a prayer, 'God be with us' (8). Isaiah follows this with an oracle in defiance of those enemies. They are still subject to God (compare 10:5–19) and will be stopped. 'Immanuel' now becomes a cry of victory, 'God *is* with us' (10b). Thus the double sense of the Immanuel sign, noted in chapter 7, of judgement and hope is again interwoven here.

Verses 11–15 show how Isaiah was preserved from the general panic and political faithlessness of his people by direct revelation from God. The verbs of verses 12,13 are plural, showing that Isaiah was not utterly alone, but had gathered a small group of followers, those who, as exceptions to 6:10, did hear and respond. The picture of God as a Rock (14,15) was very old (see Deut. 32:4, 18, 30, 31), but here, fitting in with the context, it has a double meaning. The rock is a refuge to the obedient, but a rock of ruin to the faithless. The imagery is applied to Jesus in 1 Peter 2:8, and, in parabolic form, is applied by Jesus to himself and his teaching (Matt. 7:24–27).

If verse 16 is spoken by Isaiah, then 'my disciples' refers to his followers. But if it is spoken by God to Isaiah, then God recognises in this small band a remnant faithful to himself, who will join Isaiah in patient obedience and hope (18). Jesus' gathering of disciples to himself was a similar act, and Hebrews 2:13 uses this passage of the church, faithful, teachable and obedient (see Heb. 3).

Verses 19–22 depict the confusion to come, and the spiritual and physical chaos it will bring. Having rejected the true word of God, men turn to worthless substitutes (19, compare Deut. 18:9–12), and grope in darkness. Only the revealed, written word brings light and hope (20).

THOUGHT: 'Fear him, ye saints, and you will then have nothing else to fear' (verses 12,13).

9 The coming King

Verses 1–7. The northern provinces of Israel (Zebulun and Naphtali) were conquered and annexed by Assyria in 734–732, with much deportation. The point of verses 1,2 is thus that the place where the darkness first fell will be the place where the light of God's salvation will first dawn (see Matt. 4:12–17). The 'contempt' was because the rest of Israel reckoned the northern provinces had been totally rejected by God (see John 7:52). The prophetic hymn (1–7) has five 'stanzas': verse 1 promises the reversal of fortunes for the 'lost' provinces. Verses 2,3 swell with rejoicing, the greatest joy of an agricultural people – harvest. Verses 4,5 celebrate the reason – *God's* victory over the oppressor – with an appropriately northern reference to Gideon's victory over the Midianites (see Judg. 6, 7) and merge into a vision of the end of all war (a recurring theme in Old Testament messianic eschatology, compare Isa. 2:4; Ps. 46:9–11). Verse 6 is probably based on the 'throne-names' used in the coronation of oriental kings as the people acclaim their deliverer–king. ('child is born', 'son is given' probably originally referred to the adoption by God of the king as his 'son', compare Ps. 2:6,7; 2 Sam. 7:13,14). Verse 7 characterises the rule of the coming king as one of everlasting 'peace', which is not just absence of war, but the positive establishment of harmony through 'justice' and 'righteousness'. The concluding line of verse 7 affirms that this is no utopian dream, but the assured purpose of the God of all power.

The names of verse 6 show clearly that no ordinary Davidic king is envisaged. *'Wonderful Counsellor'*: one who will need no outside advice for his plans will be those of God himself (compare 28:29). *'Mighty God'*: the king was already regarded as God's representative on earth (compare Pss. 45:6,7; 72), but this identifies the coming king with God (compare 10:21). *'Everlasting Father'*: this speaks of his enduring rule as one of beneficient authority. *'Prince of Peace'*: reminiscent of Gideon's name for God (Judg. 6:24), and compare Psalm 72:7; Isaiah 11:6–9; Micah 5:2–5a.

Verses 8–21 form a separate oracle of judgement, which possibly originally included 5:25–30 as a final stanza. It is a retrospective look at God's past judgements and Israel's persistent failure to respond (compare also the Book of Judges, Ps. 78; Ezek. 16 and 20). Verses 8–12: no matter what God did, the people felt they could recover by human strength (10). Verses 13–17: judgement will affect every rank and stratum – even those whose 'innocence' is falsely assumed (17). Verses 18–21: even civil war is a form of God's wrath; the stanza refers to the struggle for the throne after the death of Jeroboam II. Chapter 5:25–30 has pronounced the final verdict and sentence.

THOUGHT: 'He who has been born king . . . we have come to worship him' (Matt. 2:2).

10:5–34 The rod of God's anger

God and Assyria (5–19). This bold oracle begins in the same way as the 'Woes' directed at Judah ('Ah', 5, RSV, is weak; it is 'woe to Assyria', compare NIV), but directs God's judgement at the very agent of his judgement – Assyria. Isaiah simply assumes that Assyria – the super-power of his day – is under the control of Israel's God, the Lord of history. They were only a 'stick' in God's hands to chastise his own people (5,6). But in fulfilling this divinely permitted role they even exceeded contemporary levels of brutality and greed. Therefore, once they have been used by God for *his* purpose, their arrogance will be humbled (12). Two aspects of their wickedness are evident in the words of the king of Assyria: to him the God of Jerusalem was no different from the gods of nations he had laid low (8–11) and was likely to be as powerless. Viewed from his standpoint, we might excuse him for thinking thus – but verses 13 and 14 reveal both his immense arrogance and the grasping, thieving mentality that fuelled his imperialism. Such aggressive trampling on the weak inevitably aroused the wrath of the Guardian of human rights. Such boasting calls only for ridicule (15, compare the New Testament condemnation of boasting Rom. 3:27; 1 Cor. 1:29; 3:21; 4:7). The punishment decreed in verses 16–19 mixes the metaphors of wasting fever and forest fire – the former corresponding to the actual event (compare 2 Kings 19:35).

The remnant (20–23). The name of Isaiah's son (7:3) again forms the basis of a prophecy of dual significance. *Only* a remnant will be left after the righteous judgement of God (22, 23). But that remnant will be thoroughly converted to trust in *God*, no longer in unstable political alliances (20,21). The idea of 'return' is not, therefore, limited to physical return to the land, but includes spiritual 'turning back' to the Lord. It is in fact the Old Testament word for repentance and conversion (compare Pss. 80:3, 7, 18, 19; 85:4; Isa. 45:22).

A call to trust (24–34). The message that Assyria is under God's control issues in an appeal for faith. Verses 24–27 reinforce this appeal by reminding the people of God's past deliverance from what had been an equally irresistible foe – Midian (see Judg. 6:1–6). Verses 28–32, however, throw faith into the furnace of terror. The lightning-fast invasion of the Assyrian army to within a mile and a half from Jerusalem (Nob, 32) is described with appalling vividness. But God will act with even greater speed and devastation (33,34). He is not taken by surprise! But will his people trust him in their terror?

THOUGHT: This chapter should help us keep the 'Assyrias' of our day in divine perspective. Turn verse 24 into a prayer for Christians suffering oppression.

11 The age to come

The Messianic King (1–5). 'The stump of Jesse' means that the line of Davidic kings would be cut off, as happened in the next century, but just as Israel itself would survive judgement in a remnant (6:13), so there would be a future king to fulfil the promises made to David. With this prophecy of a Davidic king, compare Jeremiah 23:5,6 and Ezekiel 37:24–28. The quality of his rule (3b–5) is preceded by his character (2), upon which it depends. Like David, he is anointed by the Spirit of God (compare 1 Sam. 16:13), which will equip him intellectually, effectively, and spiritually (the three couplets of verse 2). Note the correspondence to the prime virtues of the Wisdom literature (see Prov. 1:1–7). His rule not only combines the ideal standards for Israelite kings (compare Ps. 72), but hints at a greater than human insight (3b, contrast 1 Sam. 16:7b). Note: 4b refers to his judicial verdicts. His rule will be characterised by righteousness because he himself is in a perfectly 'right' relationship with God, as verse 3a reveals. The principal beneficiaries of his rule will be the weak and defenceless (4a).

The Messianic Age (6–9). The important link between this superb vision and the foregoing is that when righteousness prevails among men under the rule of the king, then the whole natural order will be transformed by a restoration of harmony, trust and peace. The significant point is not merely the removal of animal violence, but the end of what is harmful to man – to his cattle and children (the weak and defenceless, again). But it is verse 9b that provides the only circumstances in which such a restoration can take place, circumstances which echo verse 2 and can only be established by God himself. This kind of Old Testament prophecy, with its 'earthiness', should not just be 'spiritualised' away as an idyllic metaphor for 'heaven'. The redemption and re-creation of the whole of creation is part of the glory of the Christian hope. Compare Romans 8:19–23 and the prospect of a 'new heaven and a new earth' (2 Pet. 3:13; Rev. 21:1, based on Isaiah 65:17–25).

The Messianic people (10–16). Here, as so often in Old Testament prophecy, the nearer historical future (the actual return from exile) is interwoven with the ultimate future (for the language of ingathering compare 2:2–4). Those, however, among the nations of earth who refuse the salvation offered through the Messiah (10), will themselves be rejected and destroyed (14). Freed from fighting one another (13), the people of God will do battle with their true enemies (compare Jas. 4:1, 7).

THOUGHT: 'Fight we the fight with sorrow and sin
to set their captives free,
That the earth may be filled with the glory of God
as the waters cover the sea.'

12 Sing a new song

Those who experience the blessings of salvation prophesied in the last chapter will exult in song to God. The song begins with an acknowledgment of the justice of God's punishment (a feature of Israelite judicial practice – compare Josh. 7:19). The righteousness of God is to be praised no less for the destruction of evil than for the salvation of his people. But now, the anger which has hung inexorably over Judah (5:25; 9:12, 17, 21; 10:4) is at last turned away.

In view of the references to the Exodus from Egypt and predictions of a new Exodus in 11:15, this song appropriately echoes the Song of Moses after the Red Sea deliverance: compare verse 2 with Exodus 15:2, and verse 5a with Exodus 15:21a. The songs of the redeemed have a dynamic continuity, for though his acts of salvation have been many, there is only one Saviour God. The song of the saints in glory is the 'song of Moses and . . . of the Lamb' (Rev. 15:3).

Verse 2 not only beautifully sums up what had been the message of Isaiah in the troubled years of the previous chapters – especially the characteristic second line (see 7:4) – but is a kind of autographical play upon the meaning of his own name, Isaiah: 'The Lord is salvation'. The 'wells of salvation' (3) is a delightful image, perhaps alluding to the blessing of Jerusalem's favoured water-supply, but certainly implying both the life-giving provision and the ever-renewable resources of the salvation of God. Such imagery was given its richest exposition by the Messiah himself at the side of a well (John 4:13, and compare John 7:37,38). Interestingly, the woman to whom Jesus then spoke went on to fulfil verse 4 by 'making known his deeds'!

Verse 4 combines phrases from Psalms 105:1 and 148:13, and would therefore have reminded any Israelite of the content of both Psalms – the deeds of God in history and his sovereign lordship over all creation. The double emphasis on the *name* of God summarises this, for God's name symbolised his revelation of himself in history and nature, and also, when 'called upon', guaranteed God's saving presence among his people. Accordingly, the song reaches its climax in a burst of unbounded joy at what, for the people of God, is the supreme blessing of all, indeed it is the whole purpose of God for his whole creation: the presence of God in the midst of his people (6).

The reign of God has already begun in Christ. Therefore we can join in singing this song now, even while we wait for the consummation of his kingdom.

THOUGHT: The link between singing and strength (2b) is not just fanciful! Think of Paul and Silas in prison (Acts 16:25). It depends on the content of the song!

Questions for further study and discussion on Isaiah 7–12

1. How may we 'use the word of God to justify disobedience to the command of God' (see notes on Isa. 7)?

2. Why was Ahaz condemned for refusing to ask for a sign (7:10–16)? When is it right to ask for a sign?

3. Isaiah, like Jesus, gathered a group of followers (see notes on Isa. 5). A group might like to role play a conversation with someone who says, 'I can be a Christian by myself. I don't need to go to church' (compare Heb. 10:25). What are the dangers of trying to be a Christian in isolation?

4. Do you find any continuing relevance in the Immanuel prophecies of chapters 7 and 8, or is their significance exhausted by Matthew's use of 7:14?

5. In the light of 8:19,20, what would you say to anyone who asks your advice about Spiritualism?

6. Outline those features of the person and work of Christ, past, present and future, which can be related to the messianic prophecies of 9:2–7 and 11:1–5.

7. How would you make the theme of God's control of world history (ch. 10) relevant today?

8. See note on 11:6–9. Do you agree that this kind of prophecy should not simply be 'spiritualised away'?

13 Judgement on Babylon

We now begin a section of the book (chapters 13–23) containing oracles about foreign nations (though chapter 22 is about Jerusalem). From an early period, Israelite prophecy had not been confined to Israel alone, but was concerned with persons and events in surrounding nations. The ministry of Elisha illustrates this, and the book of Amos, the earliest written collection of prophecy, begins with a catalogue of judgement 'abroad' before 'homing in' on Israel. This world-wide vision underlines the universal sovereignty claimed, on the basis of revelation, by Israel for their God. It is the prophetic version of the moral conviction of the Psalmist (Ps. 33:13–15).

The list begins with Babylon, for it was Babylon who, in the century after Isaiah, would destroy Jerusalem and take captive the people of God. Babylon, therefore, as well as being the historic enemy of Israel, destined for historical destruction herself, became the symbol of all human opposition to God and her judgement became the symbol of God's final judgement of the earth. In this chapter the two themes are closely interwoven.

The noise and commotion of battle begins the scene (verses 2–5). An army is being mustered. Only at verse 4b are we told who the Commander is – 'the LORD of hosts' (a name of God with military origins, and a favourite of Isaiah). But though the target is understood (from verse 1) to be Babylon, the vision expands quickly to describe God's judgement of the whole earth (5b, compare 11). Such is the Day of the Lord (compare Amos 5:18–20). But the cosmic upheavals here described (10, 13, compare Matt. 24:29) are not wanton destruction, but a discriminatory purging away of 'sinners' (9) and all that is wicked and arrogant (11). Nevertheless, the awfulness of God's wrath is painted in the horrific imagery of ancient warfare (13–16).

Verse 17 brings us back to the historical overthrow of Babylon, which was to take place in 539 BC at the hands of the Medes, partners in the Medo-Persian empire of Cyrus. But though the Medes are the human agents, Isaiah maintains the same insistence as in chapter 10 that they are the instrument of God (17). Babylon thus joins Sodom and Gomorrah as an archetype of human pride laid low by God (19). The symbol is revived in Revelation 18. The predictions of verses 20–22 were realised when the city was eventually abandoned in the late fourth century BC and became an uninhabited wilderness.

THOUGHT: the sombreness of this chapter highlights even more the salvation of chapter 12. What should be our practical response? Ponder 2 Peter 3:10–13.

14:1–27 'How the mighty are fallen . . !'

Verses 1–3 describe the *great reversal* that would take place when the power of Babylon was broken. The historical decree of Cyrus (see Ezra 1) enabled this prophecy to be fulfilled, but again, the motive cause is the Lord's compassionate grace (compare 40:1), and his gift of 'rest' (3; compare how the theme of rest recurs in Scripture: Heb. 3:11–4:11).

Verses 4–21 are a *taunt song* against the defeated king of Babylon – probably referring to the whole dynasty rather than any particular king. It has two parts, introduced by 'How . . .': verses 4–11 celebrate the breaking of his oppression; verses 12–21, the humbling of his pride. In the first half relief and joy (7) at the cessation of his relentless oppression are the dominant feelings on earth, even in nature (8). Meanwhile, in the land of the dead, the great king is greeted by past generations of tyrants. Death has reduced them all to pathetic, shadowy weakness (10). The intrinsic rottenness of the king of Babylon's earthly glory receives its ghastly physical counterpart (and counterpane) in the grave (11). The second half begins with an account of his presumptuous self-exaltation, which has echoes of the Babel story (Gen. 11:1–9), but is perhaps based on some ancient myth of how the rising morning star sought to climb higher than any other but was cast down by the sun. The Latin name for the morning star, 'Lucifer': 'Light-bringer' (see AV), coupled with the saying of Jesus in Luke 10:18 has led this passage to be understood as the description of Satan's original sin of presumption and his casting down. But Jesus' saying clearly refers to the success of his disciples' proclamation of the Kingdom of God, and it is precarious to build any doctrine of Satan on this text which explicitly refers to a human figure. Nevertheless, 1 Timothy 3:6 and the nature of the tempting of Eve do support the view that presumptuous usurping of divine prerogative is the 'fingerprint' of Satan. Again, the shattering contrast emerges in verse 15: from pretentious heights to the deepest darkness. Verses 16–21 describe 'a fate worse than death', in the ancient world, namely lack of proper burial (19) – all the more shameful for a king (18) – and loss of posterity (21). Verse 21 may be an echo of the fate of Zedekiah at the hands of Nebuchadnezzar (2 Kings 25:6, 7). The horrific power of this poem is reinforced by the epilogue, spoken by God himself (22, 23).

Verses 24–27 are *a detached oracle* against Assyria, similar to 10:5–34, predicting defeat at the hands of God (25) for the humanly invincible. The emphasis on 'my purpose' is a taunting echo of the Assyrian's own cocksure intentions (10:7).

THOUGHT: In contrast to the self-asserting pretended divinity of this figure, ponder the self-emptying true deity of Christ (Phil. 2:6–11).

14:28–16:14 Philistia and Moab

Against Philistia (14:28–32). Apart from the circumstance noted in verse 28, the background to this oracle is somewhat obscure. Ahaz had been pro-Assyrian. His death and the accession of Hezekiah led to a reversal of that policy, which coincided with a temporary weakening of Assyrian power. Apparently an embassy from the Philistines came to Jerusalem (32a), perhaps to get Judah to join an anti-Assyrian alliance. Isaiah's answer was to predict a revival of the Assyrian threat (29), which would destroy the Philistines (30b, 31). Characteristically, he counselled Israel to trust solely in the God of Zion (32b).

Concerning Moab (15:1–16:14). This is an oracle which is said to have been re-used here (16:13), and is again quoted and amplified in Jeremiah 48. So it is impossible to relate it with certainty to any known event in the history of Moab – a neighbour of Israel, regarded as a 'relative' (Gen 19:36,37), but also as an ancestral foe (Deut. 23:3,4). Chapter 15 vividly describes a sudden and devastating invasion by night (whether it is in prediction or 'reporting' is not apparent, but 16:14 makes the former more possible). The over-running of the whole country is pictured in the terror of the named cities and villages – Kir (1b) being the chief southern stronghold. Its fate sealed Moab's doom. Then follows the heart-rending vision of the stream of refugees fleeing southwards in grief and terror (5), clutching the remains of their possessions (7) – the universal victims of warfare in all ages.

Chapter 16 opens with the refugees uneasily encamped in Edom, of which Sela was the famous rock-fortress capital. But from there they send an entreaty, accompanied by a token tribute (lambs, verse 1), to Jerusalem to ask for more secure protection. Unfortunately it is not clear who speaks in verses 3–5. If this is the *Moabites'* request, then the messianic 4b,5 are odd, and verses 6,7 would have to be understood as a refusal to help. But if these verses are God's instructions to Jerusalem, then compassionate protection for the suffering is commanded, even though the actual judgement is deserved and will be catastrophic (6–12). The people of God may not avert his judgements upon men in history, but the punishment should evoke grief, not gloating (15:5; 16:9, 11). There should be a practical response of caring justice – in the light of our expectation of God's kingdom of peace and righteousness (4b,5).

THOUGHT: With these chapters compare Proverbs 24:17 and 25:21.

17:1–18:7 Syria, Israel and Ethiopia

Concerning Syria and Israel (17:1–14). The fact that Syria and Israel, the Northern Kingdom, are combined in this chapter almost certainly dates it to the early period of Isaiah's ministry, at the time of the Syrian–Israelite alliance described in chapter 7. Both kingdoms suffered under Assyria. In 732 Damascus was conquered, and in 721 Israel, after being reduced in territory at that time (compare 'will grow lean', verse 4), was conquered and Samaria destroyed. The pictures of verses 5,6 aptly describe Assyria's policy of systematic destruction of vassal nations by deportation and dispersion. One reason for Israel's judgement is given in verses 8, 10,11 – their addiction to idolatry. Verses 10b and 11 probably refer to gardens with swift-growing plants, which as quickly died, cultivated in honour of Canaanite dying and rising gods of fertility. Such practices are seen as pathetic in contrast with the living God of Israel, the Creator and Holy One (8a), the God of their history of deliverance and constant protection (10a). The barb of this oracle is that by lumping Israel with Damascus and including her in the oracles against foreign nations, the prophet implies that when the people of God abandon him they forfeit their relationship with him and join the ranks of the objects of his judgement. They become, indeed, no better than the original inhabitants of the land. Like them, they shall be driven out for their sins (9). Yet even the severest harvesting leaves a few gleanings (6), and God will salvage the faithful few who worship him alone (7). The Chronicler records an initial fulfilment of this in the later days of Hezekiah (2 Chron. 30:10,11, 25). Meanwhile, the ravages of the Assyrian will eventually come to nought. Verses 12–14 offer reassurance for Jerusalem, and are drawn from the language of Psalms 46 and 93. With verse 14 compare again 37:36.

Concerning Ethiopia (18:1–7). Another reply to ambassadors (2, compare 14:28–32), this time from Ethiopia–Sudan (Heb. 'Cush' – the land south of Egypt which at this time was in political control over Egypt), who were seeking Judah's alliance against Assyria. Again Isaiah's reply (2b–7) is simple refusal, based on complete trust in God's dependability (4) timing and power (5). Verse 7 looks beyond the historical crisis, and sees in the Ethiopian envoys examples of the ingathering of all nations to the dwelling place of God, in fulfilment of 2:3.

THOUGHT: In the daily temptation to rely on the 'work of our own hands', we need the challenge of 17:10a.

19 Egypt: judgement and conversion

This is one of the most remarkable chapters in the Old Testament. Beginning with a prophecy of catastrophe for Egypt (1–15), it concludes with a breathtaking vision of God's blessing on his former arch-enemies, Egypt and Assyria.

The oracle of woe upon Egypt cannot be related with certainty to any particular set of historical circumstances. It breaks into three stanzas.

Verses 1–4 describe the social dissolution of Egypt. The first victims of God's approach are the gods – whose impotence had already been demonstrated at the time of the Exodus. Thus the spiritual and moral strength of the people melts away (1). That is followed by civil strife (2), by panic and confusion (3) and finally tyranny (4).

Verses 5–10, with considerable detail, envisage the economic collapse of the country. The failure of the Nile floods will mean ruin for irrigation and agriculture (6,7), fisheries (8), and the linen and cotton export trade (9). The social consequences will hurt every class in society (10).

Verses 11–15 complete the picture of utter confusion, in which even the Egyptian wise men – the most famous in the world – are at a loss. Zoan and Memphis were important cities of Egypt.

The remainder of the chapter adds five further oracles concerning Egypt, which combine probable historical allusions with expectations of a Day of the Lord that will be nothing short of a transformation of history. The 'fear' of the Israelites (16,17) is an allusion to the panic in Egypt that preceded the Exodus (Exod. 12:29–36). Verse 18 accurately predicts the later existence of Jewish colonies in Egypt, though the identification of the cities is impossible. 'City of the Sun' is one of several variant readings for the Hebrew 'City of Destruction'. It perhaps refers to Heliopolis. Verses 19–22 look beyond the present judgement to the establishing of a witness to the true God in Egypt with the result that the Egyptians will be fully converted to him. Verse 20 even applies the language of the Exodus to the Egyptians themselves! Verse 22 reveals the gracious purpose behind judgement – a purpose that will ultimately produce fellowship between implacable enemies (23). Egypt and Assyria have here become 'typical' rather than literal. The blessing of God upon Israel will be for the rest of the world (as promised to Abraham). The Gentiles too will be 'my people', 'my handiwork'. The fulfilment of this began in the New Testament in the reconciling work of Christ (compare Eph. 2:11–22) and the universal mission of the church (compare 1 Pet. 2:9,10).

THOUGHT: If we see in verses 1–15 an apt word of judgement on contemporary society, let us also see in verses 19–25 a stimulus to pray for the 'healing' hand of God and his reign of peace and blessing.

20:1–21:17 The oppressor destroyed

The folly of trust in Egypt (20:1–6). Between 713–711 BC the northerly Philistine city of Ashdod rebelled against Assyria, hoping for support from the Ethiopian-Egyptian empire, and seeking to draw Judah into the revolt. Isaiah's powerful persuasion had prevented that. Now, in 711, when the Assyrians crushed the revolt and the Egyptian help had not materialised, the full meaning of Isaiah's action was made clear, and his warnings vindicated. This kind of prophetic acted symbolism was a common method of reinforcing the message. Often it was at considerable personal cost to the prophet (for example, Ezekiel), but on this occasion it bought the survival of Jerusalem.

The fall of Babylon 21:1–10: This is a powerful visionary oracle against a nation first given a symbolic title (1a) that implies desolation and chaos, only later identified as **Babylon** (9). The prophet is 'projected' into the sixth century to the point when the Babylonian oppressor of the Judean exiles was about to be overwhelmed by the Medo-Persian empire (2b). In this way God would bring to an end the 'sighing' of his exiled people (2b), but the violence and totality of the events (1b, 2a) fill the prophet with intense physical horror (3). The overthrow of their enemies was 'longed for', but the actual fulfilment of it was a cause of 'trembling' (4). We have met this prophetic grief over the fate of the wicked in chapters 15–16. Even Sodom had its Abraham to intercede. How unlike the sullen anger of Jonah at God's mercy on Nineveh (Jonah 4)! Verse 5 probably pictures the Babylonian court unsuspectingly revelling in its luxury at the time of the attack (compare Dan. 5). In verse 6 the prophet 'splits himself', as it were, into both a watchman and one who waits for news. The 'riders' of verses 7 and 9 are perhaps the victorious army, or the fugitives of the defeated, or even the returning exiles. At any rate, their significance is beyond doubt. The cry of 9b brings sweet news to the longsuffering ('threshed . . .') people of God, who are assured in verse 10 of the objective certainty of the vision.

Concerning Edom. Verses 11, 12 ('Dumah' means 'Silence', and is probably a word-play on Edom; Seir was a common name for Edom) continue the watchman theme. The watchman is asked how much of the night (? foreign domination) is left before morning (deliverance). His answer is ambiguous.

Concerning Arabia. Verses 13–17 indicate the farthest extent of Assyrian conquest – even to desert tribes.

THOUGHT: Are we ever apalled at the overthrow of the wicked, which is part of what we pray for as we glibly say: 'Thy kingdom come . . .'?

22 An unheeded lesson

Concerning Jerusalem (1–14, symbolically called 'the valley of vision', that is, the place of Isaiah's prophesying). The setting of this oracle is the joyful relief in the city following the collapse of Sennacherib's siege in 701. Though Isaiah had foretold the deliverance, he neither joined in nor approved of the wild rejoicing (1b, 2a). Firstly, this was because he saw how serious had been the deprivation and loss of life in the siege and among those who had tried to escape (2b, 3; compare 1:7–9). But secondly, he foresaw the later destruction of the city by the Babylonians, which happened in 587. The violence of his vision (5–8) caused him intense grief (4) which made the city's transient jollity all the more intolerable. And thirdly, he refused to rejoice because the revelry betrayed an utter lack of penitence (12–14). The Assyrian invasion and siege was a lesson which should have shocked the people to repentance (12), but they would not understand that (compare 1:3–6) and celebrated defiantly (13). Such total impenitence can only meet total un-forgiveness (14). In verses 8b–11 Isaiah foresees the inhabitants falling back into their inveterate habit – faithless reliance on their own ability to save themselves. 'House of the Forest': a name for the king's palace which probably incorporated an armoury. Weapons, walls and water were all they thought they needed. But the God they were ignoring had other plans (11b). Are we any better when it comes to trusting God rather than our paltry self-defences?

Concerning Shebna and Eliakim (15–25). 'This steward . . . over the household' refers to the highest official over the king's palace – a highly responsible and prestigious post. The passionate attack on its current holder showed that neither the Lord nor his prophet were dazzled by human pomp. Shebna may have been a foreigner with no legal right to own land for a tomb (16), but it is likely that the tomb building was but the culmination of a characteristic pride and show (compare 'splendid chariots', 18), which was a 'pet-hate' of Isaiah (see 2:12–17). He is careful, however, to make clear that the prediction of a violent expulsion is a word of the Lord (15a), not personal vindictiveness. His successor, Eliakim, would ultimately be the victim of his own success, pulled down by the weight of nepotism and patronage (24). 'The key of the house of David . . . to open . . . and shut' (22) meant the power to make decisions, subject only to the king himself, but always accountable to him as steward. This was the nature of the power entrusted by Jesus the King to Peter and the church (Matt. 16:19; 18:18).

CHECK POINT for oneself and one's church: 'Activism . . . a denial of faith (9–11); escapism . . . a denial of repentance (12–14)' (Kidner).

23 Tyre, multi-national harlot

The oracles against foreign nations began with Babylon, the oppressor (ch. 13). They end here with Tyre, the seductress. The two cities, symbolic respectively of politico-military and economic imperialism, are climactically combined in Revelation 17 and 18. The Phoenician trading empire, from its two great ports, Tyre and Sidon, stretched to the boundaries of the known world. Its collapse, therefore, would be far reaching in its effects, and this chapter ranges to and fro around the trade routes, from Cyprus, their nearest colony, to Tarshish (probably Tartessos in Southern Spain). It would be especially felt in Egypt whose corn trade passed through Tyre and Sidon (3, 5). The shame of conquest is compared to childlessness (4); it is a 'shame' because of the reversal of her colonising power and prestige (7, 8). Verse 10 possibly envisages far–off colonies rebelling in the absence of imperial 'restraint'. The human force responsible is identified in verse 13. The Chaldeans were one of a series of powers who successively attacked and partially subdued the Phoenicians. But behind them lay the ultimate purpose of God (9–12), a purpose in line with his opposition to all human arrogance and self-sufficiency (compare 2:10–22).

Such was the resilience of Tyre, however, that she recovered a generation or so after each disaster. This is the general meaning of the round figure 'seventy years' of verses 15–17. It is noteworthy, however, that roughly such a period did pass between the most successful conquest of Tyre, by Alexander the Great in 332 BC, and its restoration in 274 by Ptolemy II. But the prophet douses any glory such a revival might generate by comparing it to the renewed activity of a forgotten prostitute. The metaphor of seduction with the lure of economic growth, trade and 'multi-national' (17b) expansion is a powerful one and perennially relevant (compare Rev. 18:3).

All the more surprising, therefore, is the last verse which foretells that ultimately all this economic wealth and produce will enrich the people of God. This has to be seen in the context of the expected transformation of the world and society that God will effect in the new age of salvation. This inclusion of the fruit of man's economic activity, transformed and redeemed, in the Kingdom of God is a feature of the Old Testament hope (compare Ps. 72:10; Isa. 18:7, 45:14; Hag. 2:7) which is not lost sight of in the New Testament (see Rev. 21:24).

THOUGHT: 'Blessed are the meek, for they shall inherit the earth' (Matt. 5:5).

Questions for further study and discussion on Isaiah 13–23

1. Think about the plight of refugees in the world today. Who and where are they? What is happening to them? What does the Bible say about their situation (see, for instance, notes on 14:28–16:14).

2. How do you react to the basic theme of judgement in these chapters? On what principles does God's judgement operate?

3. Using a concordance, make a study of 'Babylon' as a historical city and as a symbolic term in Scripture.

4. Considering Babylon (chs. 13; 14) and Tyre (ch. 23) as representatives respectively of political and economic forms of oppression and exploitation, what current examples of such forces do you see as within the 'field of relevance' of these oracles?

5. Discuss your experience of the 'daily temptation to rely on the "work of our own hands" '. How can we overcome this (see notes on 17–18:7)?

6. Are there modern parallels to the features of dissolution of Egypt painted in chapter 19?

7. Compose a portrait of 'pride' – national, cultural and individual – based on its frequent appearance in these chapters.

8. Why did Isaiah act out his prophecy (Isa. 20)? What role should or could drama play in our Christian teaching and worship?

24 Cosmic judgement

Chapters 24–27, often known as *The Apocalypse of Isaiah*, are another self-contained section within the book. The prophet's gaze widens from specific foreign nations to the whole world. 'Apocalyptic' is the name given to a class of literature devoted mainly to visionary and often symbolic description of the ultimate future. The word means 'revealing what is hidden'. The major biblical examples, apart from these chapters of Isaiah, are Daniel, Zechariah and Revelation, and the apocalyptic sayings of Jesus (Mark 13, Matt. 24). Dominant themes in this kind of literature are the sovereign control of God over history, the certain destruction of the wicked and a call to the righteous to endure oppression and tribulation in the light of the vindication and deliverance that will come when God intervenes at the end of the age.

In this chapter God's judgement on the whole earth is depicted with tremendous poetic power (the Hebrew is full of repetition, alliteration, rhyme and word-play). Verses 1–3 combine the awful force of the judgement (1, 3) with its universality. No one will be able to claim exemption on grounds of privilege or of poverty (2). Verses 4–6 reinforce the intimate connection between human moral evil and fracture in the natural order (Gen. 3). Man's 'pollution' of the earth (4) was particularly related to the shedding of blood (Num. 35:33, but also to adultery and idolatry, compare Jer. 3:2, 9). This was a breaking of the 'everlasting covenant' made with mankind through Noah which specifically singles out the sanctity of life (Gen. 9:1–17). A similar emphasis, using similar concepts, is found in Hosea 4:1–10, which may have been the inspiration behind this chapter. Verses 7–13 show the effect of the judgement of drought – thirst, absence of wine, and the end of all joy (compare Joel 1). Those who were accustomed to revelry, perhaps in spite of God's warnings, are warned of the desolation to come. Verses 14–16 are an abrupt change of mood, referring to the reverse side of God's judgement – the rejoicing of his redeemed people, gathered from the ends of the earth (the vision therefore includes Gentiles as well as Jews). The joy is in praise of God, not over the fate of the wicked, whose present behaviour is rather a cause of pain to the prophet (16b). Verses 17–23 reach a terrifying climax depicting the inescapability of the judgement because it will be cosmic in extent. 'The host of heaven' (21) can mean the stars, but probably here denotes the spiritual hosts of evil, alongside their earthly counterparts. In the end, only God will reign in glory (23).

THOUGHT: This chapter must surely enhance our appreciation of the desolation Christ bore for us and our gratitude for the glorious truth of Romans 8:1.

25 The messianic banquet

We have already seen the downfall of particular cities – especially Babylon and Tyre, representative respectively of political and economic oppression. This chapter opens with song of praise (1–5) for God's overthrow of 'the city' – which probably bears a general, representative sense here, that is, the city as embodying all that opposes God and that oppresses his people. The prophet sees the time when this 'urban rebellion' (which goes back to Cain, compare Gen. 4:16,17) will be not only shattered, but reversed and transformed into a source of glory to God (3). That is why God chooses a *city*, Jerusalem, as the place where his name dwells. Jerusalem becomes the focus and symbol of this hope, appearing as God's city in the great visions of the established Kingdom of God (Rev. 21–22, compare Ezek. 48:35b). Meanwhile, however, the blast of oppression continues to scorch and batter (4). Only in God is there protection, security and hope. The vision of a future salvation is guaranteed by the experience of God's past deeds, and confidence in his 'faithful and sure' plans (1). (For an excellent treatment of the theme of 'the city' in Scripture, see Jacques Ellul: *The Meaning of the City*, Eerdmans, 1970.)

The picture of the age of salvation as a great banquet (6) is one that not only exudes joy, but also fulfilment after anxious waiting (as of harvest festival), of relief after labour, and of shared, communal enjoyment. Jesus used it not only in parable (Luke 14:15–24), but also as the ultimate 'reference point' of the sacramental feast – the Lord's Supper (Luke 22:16, 18; Matt. 26:29). We note again the world-wide extent of this hope. The Lord's feast will bring 'all people' into table-fellowship with himself and each other (compare Matt. 8:11). Verses 7, 8 show that salvation will not only be world–wide in extent, but total in effect, by reaching to the worst and final enemy – death itself. The 'covering' and 'veil' could refer to spiritual blindness, but are more likely in this context to refer to the covered face of the bereaved mourner. The Lord will remove the veil of mourning, and wipe away the tears underneath, for their cause will have been destroyed. Verse 8 is a triumphant Old Testament prophecy that the New Testament echoes abundantly in the light of the resurrection of Jesus (compare 1 Cor. 15:54–57; Rev. 7:17; 21:4), which gives substance to the expectant waiting of verse 9.

The dark side of salvation is not forgotten, however. The pervasive Isaianic theme of pride laid low is repeated in the fate of Moab – as degrading as it is final (10–12).

THOUGHT: Do our communion services evoke anything of the joy of the messianic banquet to which they point?

26 Peace in the storm

'A strong city' (1–6). These verses envisaging the secure city for God's redeemed people form a counterpart to 25:1–5. The emphasis is on the city's enduring safety, because it is God who establishes it (1). Only the righteous will inhabit it (2), but who are 'the righteous'? Not those who exalt their own works, but those who trust solely in God (3,4). Verse 3 (compare Ps. 112:7) indicates what 'trust' means – namely a deliberate act of fixing one's mind (and will) upon God, that is, of relating every thought, plan, action and desire back to him as the foundation (4). 'Peace', therefore, is not just absence of strife, but the wholeness and security that come from such a habit.

Trust in the midst of distress (7–18). The quality of the trust just described is here seen supporting the community in the midst of the tribulations of the last days. The prayer begins with a confident affirmation (7), even though circumstances may seem to deny it (compare the same feature in Ps. 73). 'Thy memorial name' (8) means the remembrance and proclamation of God's name (signifying his person and power) in public worship – something the fervent worshipper longs to see extended to the whole earth (9–11) in order that moral chaos may be banished and the Lord himself acknowledged. Verses 13–15 show the confidence of the people that even under foreign domination ('other lords' means human tyrants, not false gods), the people of God prosper. Christians under persecution prove the truth of this. Again we note that 'peace' (12) is what God gives *in* the storm, not just *after* it! Nevertheless, for all their ultimate confidence in God, the people are overwhelmed by a sense of frustration at their own impotence and the apparent delay in God's intervention (18b) – as though all the labours of childbirth were futile (18a). This is the cue for God to speak:

The hope of resurrection and safety in judgement (19–21). Verse 19 is one of the only two unambiguous prophecies of bodily resurrection in the Old Testament (the other is Dan. 12:2). It is the voice of God claiming for himself even the dead of his people ('their bodies' [RSV] is an emendation; the Hebrew reads, 'my bodies'). Death is seen as sleep; those in the grave ('dwellers in the dust') will be awakened to refreshment ('dew') and joy. Verses 20, 21 conclude with the assurance of comfort and protection for God's people in the final judgement. How much more can we rely on it in our lesser, present trials!

THOUGHT: 'Stayed upon Jehovah, hearts are fully blest;
Finding, as he promised, perfect peace and rest.'

27 The great homecoming

Verse 1 completes the judgement oracle of the previous verse by predicting the final destruction of evil itself – pictured here under the guise of the great sea-monster, Leviathan, drawn from Canaanite mythology. Israel used the pictures of that mythology in ways which exalted the sovereign power and victory of the Lord (compare 30:7, 51:9; Job 26:12; Ps. 74:13). As in 24:21, the judgement upon evil men and nations is completed by the destruction of the spiritual power of evil that lies behind them, which is probably what the symbol of Leviathan here stands for, rather than a disguised reference to any particular nation. This kind of imagery reaches its climax in the 'beast from the sea' in Revelation 13.

Verses 2–6 reverse the vineyard song of 5:1–7. After the judgement the Lord will tend his vineyard (3), so that its fruit, which 5:7 showed us was righteousness and justice, will be enjoyed world-wide (6). Verses 4,5 are somewhat obscure, but suggest that God will endure no further encroachment or disturbance of his precious work (4), yet would prefer the repentance and reconciliation of his enemies to their destruction (5).

Verses 7–11 are difficult, but their main point appears to be a contrast between the limited punishment upon God's own people, for the purpose of purification (7–9), and the total destruction of those who refuse him (10,11). Verse 7 is a question arising out of the prediction that Israel's oppressors would themselves be destroyed (compare 10:5–19). Was Israel then to suffer the same fate? No, the Exile would serve the purpose of atoning for their sins (compare 40:2), and purging them of idolatry (9). The judgement was utterly real and very severe (8, compare the tone of Lamentations), but purposeful and bounded by forgiveness. ('Measure by measure' [8a] is a guess at an unknown Hebrew word, which might mean 'by shooing away', as of animals). By contrast, the wicked cut themselves off totally from God's compassion by two things: (*a*) their persistence in rebellion, as implied in 'the *fortified* city' (10), and (*b*) their wilful blindness in refusing to acknowledge God their Creator (11b, compare 44:18–20; Rom. 1:19–32).

Verses 12,13 return to the figure of fruit and harvest in order to picture the great ingathering of God's people. The gathering is seen in all its splendour in Revelation 7. The great 'Apocalypse of Isaiah' thus ends on a heartening note – '*Home at last!*'

THOUGHT: How is God's appeal to the wicked in verse 5 to be got through to them? Paul gives his answer in 2 Corinthians 5:20.

28 True security

After the interludes of the oracles against the nations (chapters 13–23), and the apocalyptic chapters (24–27), we are back, for the remainder of this half of the book, in the troubled times of the Assyrian threat.

Chapter 28 opens with an oracle directed against the capital ('crown') of the Northern Kingdom of Israel ('Ephraim') – that is, Samaria (1–6) – described as beautiful, but besotted (compare Amos 2:12; 4:1; 6:6). The fall which will be its judgement is yet to come (2), so this oracle was given before the fall of Samaria to Assyria in 722/1. The reason for its inclusion here is to lead into a similar accusation of drunkenness against the Judean religious leaders – 'these also' (7).

Verses 7–13 are probably a direct encounter between Isaiah and those he vividly describes in verses 7,8. Verses 9,10 give his opponents' mocking reply, asking Isaiah if he thinks they are children, learning their alphabet from him (v. 10 is a mockery of Isaiah's teaching, compare NIV). To this Isaiah replies that if they will not learn from him, God will inflict an alien people on them (11). If they refuse his help (12), they will learn, by suffering, the lesson they now make fun of (13, compare verse 22).

Verses 14–22 have their background in Hezekiah's policy of alliance with Egypt against Assyria, a policy which Isaiah rejected because it betrayed lack of faith in God and because it would prove fatal anyway. Verse 15 is an example of Isaiah's use of his opponents' words to reveal the true nature of their acts. 'We have our treaty and agreement,' they say; 'with death and the grave,' adds Isaiah. 'We have a protective defence,' they say; 'based on falsehood and lies,' adds Isaiah. By contrast, the security God offers is a tested cornerstone (16). This verse has a familiar messianic interpretation (compare 1 Pet. 2:4–6), but the 'cornerstone' here is regarded in the last line as the promise of God itself. Paul, in Romans 9:33, uses the verse to highlight the necessity of faith, without which the stone becomes a stumbling-block (compare 8:14,15). '. . . be in haste' here means the confusion and shame of defeat. The useless inadequacy of human alliances remains the theme of verses 17–20. The 'strangeness' of God's deed (21) lies in the fact that the divine anger once turned against Israel's enemies (for Perazim and Gibeon compare 1 Chron. 14:11, 16) will now be turned against Israel in judgement (22).

Verses 23–29 present an agricultural parable to the effect that the changing activity of God is not capricious but is because he wants a fruitful harvest.

THOUGHT: We may stand on the promises of God, or stumble over them in unbelief. Either way, God remains a rock.

29 Zion: purged and restored

Verses 1–8 are a poem predicting both judgement on Jerusalem ('Ariel'), and its miraculous deliverance. ('Ho' [RSV] is inexplicable. The Hebrew is 'Woe to . . .'). 'Ariel' is otherwise unknown, but is usually taken to mean a 'sacrificial hearth' (compare Ezek. 43:15). Though Jerusalem keeps up its round of festivals (1b), the city itself will become a place of sacrifice (2b), its inhabitants reduced to shades (4). From verse 5 on, however, the prophecy changes, foreseeing not only the relief of the city from the historical enemy – Assyria in 701 BC – but merging into a vision of the ultimate destruction of all enemies of the City of God.

Verses 9–12 are in line with Amos 8:11,12 and Proverbs 29:18: persistent refusal of the word of the Lord will end up in its being withdrawn altogether. The prophets are the 'eyes' of the nation (10b). Without them there will be blind panic (9) and even the known word of God will appear incomprehensible (11,12). Jesus, too, was urgent about the need to respond to the word when heard: 'He who has ears to hear, let him hear (and obey)'!

Verses 13,14: The classic hypocrisy of Phariseeism brought these verses to Jesus' mind (Mark 7:6). Their relevance is not exhausted yet. None of us is beyond the temptation to let the formal and merely moral replace the genuine obedience of the heart. Israel went on 'worshipping' God, yet in practical matters refused to trust him. Their 'worship' wasn't 'worth it'.

Verses 15,16: Likewise, there is a permanence about man's delusion that he can defy God and remain undetected, absurd though it is – as the potter illustration shows (compare 45:9; 64:8).

Verses 17–22 characterise the intervention of God as a great reversal of all the evils of the present. What would have been an impossible 'natural' reversal (17) is given here to prepare us for human 'impossibilities' – in the physical realm (18), the spiritual (19), and the various social spheres about which Isaiah had earlier protested so vehemently (20, 21 – compare 1:17–23; 3:13–15; 5:8–23; 10:1, 2). It is significant for our conception of the totality of God's salvation that all these spheres of human life are so closely held together here.

Verses 22–24 envisage the joy of Jacob at the ultimate perfecting of his wayward descendants. The thought that the people who are God's own handiwork should display his glorious holiness ('sanctify my name') is richly developed in Ephesians 1:4, 6; 2:10.

THOUGHT: Unless we accept verse 24, we shall miss the 'fresh joy' of verse 19.

30:1–17 Rebellion, rejection and repentance

The 'covenant' and 'refuge' of 28:15, the secret counsel of 29:15, are now made explicit, as the alliance with Egypt, and the full extent of God's feelings about it are made plain. The key word is 'rebellious' (1, 9), for what Judah is doing is tantamount to treachery against their God. Knowing his disapproval (compare chapter 20), they had simply not consulted him, as was customary before any act of state. So Isaiah's anger is first of all aroused by the slight to his Lord. But, secondly, his own political judgement, informed by the facts of recent history, was that Egypt was a useless ally, likely to bring disaster (3–5), and certainly not worth the ludicrously laden embassy struggling through the desert to arrange the alliance (6). As a token of his contempt (7), Isaiah gives the mythical symbol for Egypt – Rahab, the turbulent sea-monster – a sarcastic nickname: 'Sits–still' ('Rahab the Do-Nothing', NIV)! This is perhaps what he was to inscribe as a public placard – a private 'demonstration' against the state policy (8).

Verses 9–11 remind us of the great opening salvo of the book (1:2–4). The persistent rejection of the word of the prophets by God's own people is such a prominent theme in Scripture that we need constantly to examine ourselves in the light of it. Amos (7:12), Jeremiah (26), and Ezekiel (33:30–33) all experienced it, as did Jesus (Luke 4:23–29), who was grieved to tears by it (Luke 13:34,35; 19:41,42). It was the whole thrust of Stephen's speech (Acts 7:51–53). Yet, as Paul perceived, in experience (Acts 13:44–47) and in doctrine (Rom. 11:11), it was used by God's sovereign providence to extend the gospel of salvation to the Gentiles, who in turn must learn its lesson (Rom. 11:20–22).

Judah would heedlessly head for destruction (13,14, 16,17) and yet the great alternative was always there – the characteristic message of Isaiah in verse 15. 'Returning' means 'repentance' – turning back to God; 'rest' means an end to futile human efforts at self-protection. It was a lesson Israel had experienced right at the beginning (Exod. 14:13, 14) but, with a few exceptions (for example, 2 Chron. 20:1–30), had never fully learned.

THOUGHT: Which part of verse 15 describes your life at present: the central promise, or the last line?

30:18–33 Mercy and judgement

Verse 18 comes as a surprise after the preceding section, but the surprise is due to our inability to conceive of God's judgement and his gracious mercy 'in the same breath'. The prophets could because they saw both as the outworking of his righteousness (18b, compare 45:8, 21b, 46:13 – where 'deliverance' in RSV translates Hebrew 'righteousness'). The tension is fully resolved only in the 'surprise' of the gospel of the Cross (Rom. 1:16,17).

Verses 19–26 continue the theme of 'reversal' from 29:17–20, firstly in the human sphere (19–22) and secondly in nature (23–26). Notes: In verse 20, 'Teacher' is a plural in Hebrew, so it could refer to the human teachers through whom God will guide his people (compare NIV) by the ministry of the Spirit (compare 1 Cor. 12:28, etc., Isa. 32:4). RSV takes it as a 'plural of majesty', referring it to God himself. In verse 21, the turning 'to the left or right' probably implies going astray, so that a voice is needed 'from behind' – that is, from the guide who calls you back to the right path. In experience, God's guidance often takes the form of preventing us pursuing *wrong* roads, rather than clearly marking out the *right* one!

Verses 27–33 portray God's judgement in terms drawn from the 'theophany' tradition (that is, of God's 'appearance' – as, for example, on Sinai, compare Exod. 19:16–20; Ps. 68:7,8). Fire and smoke were prominent symbols for his consuming but also purifying presence (compare Isaiah's own call experience, 6:1–7). 'Topheth' (33, RSV margin) was the name of the place in the valley of Hinnom, outside Jerusalem, where rubbish was burnt, but where child-sacrifices by burning later took place. Jeremiah 7:31–33 was to foresee it as a place of judgement for the people of Jerusalem but here, in the previous century, Isaiah describes it as the funeral pyre of the king of Assyria. The same place, under the name 'Gehenna', was the smouldering refuse tip that Jesus used as a picture of final destruction (see Matt. 5:29,30, 13:41,42, 49,50).

THOUGHT: We wait on the Lord for his gracious deliverance; he waits on us for our repentance (18).

31 Flight or failure?

Verses 1–3 repeat the warning of 30:1–7, but with the added detail that it was a chariot corps that the Judeans particularly requested from Egypt. The irony of verse 1 lies in associating verbs of trust, that should have applied only to God, with such items of military hardware, and overlooking the transcendent power of the 'Holy One of Israel'. 'And yet he *is* wise' (2) sarcastically implies that the people were saying, or imagining, that God was naïve in the world of politics! As if the Lord of Hosts did not understand military strategies! The critical difference is summed up in verse 3a, where it is noteworthy that the distinction between flesh and spirit is not a moral one (evil *versus* good), still less of different kinds of 'being', but rather of effective power and durability. Those who trust in anything less than God will perish along with their illusory supports (3b). Yet the people of God constantly need this reminder, for we persistently seek to build up our 'tangible' assets and resources. God may well *use* 'men and horses', but we are not to *trust* in them.

Verses 4–9. If only they would believe it, God already intended to defend Jerusalem himself – which made human help redundant (8), and any idols offensive (7, compare 30:22). All that was required of the people was a genuine repentance (6). Again we note how deeply Isaiah felt over this issue. To the Judean leaders the matter was one of practical politics – not *rejecting* the Lord, simply 'helping' him a bit! To Isaiah it was a matter of outright faithlessness amounting to revolt. Note: In verse 4 the lion probably represents God, defending his personal property ('prey' = Jerusalem) undaunted by the threats of those who were trying to rob him of it (that is, the 'shepherds' = Assyrians). Thus the second half of the verse should be interpreted as fighting for, not against, Jerusalem, in line with the picture of verse 5.

THOUGHT: 'The arm of flesh will fail you,
Ye dare not trust your own.'

Questions for further study and discussion on Isaiah 24–31

1. What criteria and principles are needed to cope with the interweaving of the prophet's contemporary situation and the 'ultimate future' in his oracles of judgement?

2. Pursue the notes on chapters 25 and 26 into a full study of the theme of 'the city' in Scripture.

3. Think about times when you have discovered God's peace in difficult circumstances (26:3,4). How has this come about for you? What is the difference between peace and apathy or lethargy?

4. What accompaniments of drunkenness are the point of complaint in chapter 28? Is it condemnation of drinking in itself?

5. Using a concordance, study the theme of 'Rock', 'stone' in Scripture (compare 28:16).

6. Compare the 'Potter' image of 29:16 with the other occasions of its use (e.g. Isa. 45:9–11, 64:8; Jer. 18:1–11; Rom. 9:19–21). What themes emerge?

7. Why are people so reluctant to face the truth in times of crisis (see, for example, 30:9–14)? How far should God's people today have a prophetic role in national crises? How should we react in the face of the rejection of our message?

8. Why was Isaiah so vehemently opposed to the Egyptian alliance? What contemporary relevance does it have for the Christian, or the church?

32 The righteous King and the outpoured Spirit

Verses 1–8. Having studied Proverbs, we shall easily recognise how much this passage is influenced by the Wisdom school. The Wisdom concern for righteous government (compare Prov. 16:10–13; 20:8, 28; 29:4, 14; 31:3–9) is here transformed into a prophecy of the messianic age of salvation in which not only will there be a righteous king (compare 7:14; 9:6,7; 11:1–5), but all subordinate authority will share his character (2). Under his influence, men will behave to one another as God does. Verse 3 envisages the reversal of 6:9,10 (and compare 29:9,10), while verse 5 answers Ecclesiastes 8:10; 10:5–7. Verses 6–8 sum up the present situation from which the messianic rule will deliver us, sifting out of familiar Wisdom themes those closest to the heart of the prophet, namely social evils. A 'compound equation' of these verses shows us that refusal or failure to meet the needs of the hungry, oppression of the poor and cynical injustice are categorised as folly, iniquity, ungodliness, error, evil and wickedness.

Verses 9–14 single out (again, compare 3:16–4:1; Amos 4:1–3) the womenfolk as typical of the sheer complacency (note the emphasis on this in verses 9–11) that coexists with such social disease (compare Ezek. 16:49). Isaiah appears to address them in the middle of their harvest festivities with his prediction of an end to such uncaring revelry.

Verses 15–20, however, return to the vision of the messianic future that will follow judgement. Significantly, therefore, in this chapter, the outpouring of the Spirit follows upon the arrival of the reign of the righteous king. The first feature of the Spirit is his life-giving, fertilising power (15, compare Ps. 104:30) transforming and transcending all natural limitations. But lest we limit this to an individualistic piety, the social effects are beautifully set out in verses 16–20. Justice and righteousness, no achievement of human effort, but the gift of God's Spirit, will produce *Shalom*, that perfect wholeness and harmony between God, man and nature, which is God's ultimate plan for his whole creation. The order is important: the initiative of God's Spirit; new life; morally transformed human relationships (justice and righteousness); peace and stability in the rest of creation.

Notes: Verse 19, perhaps displaced, is probably a further reference to the doom of the armies ('forest') of the enemy and the rebellious 'city' (compare 25:1–4). Verse 20 foresees such abundant crops that there will be no need to curtail the trampling of animals.

THOUGHT: Another beautiful image of God's purpose is in Psalm 85:10: 'Righteousness and peace will kiss each other'.

33 A celebration of deliverance

Israel had often faced military defeat and national emergency, and had an array of Psalms for such occasions (compare Pss. 20–21; 46; 68). This chapter is in similar vein, probably originally composed at the time of the Sennacherib crisis, but preserved for its relevance to future crises.

Verses 1–9 are the people's cry in distress. It includes invective against the enemy (1, 8), a plea to God (2), based on knowledge of what he has done (3,4), and on his personal greatness (5,6).

Verses 10–12 are God's initial answer, promising action for deliverance. There is a hint in verse 11 that men are self-destructive in their evil desires (compare the same thought in a different metaphor in 30:13). But the fiery judgement of God will not be confined to the enemies 'outside'; verse 14 envisages it purifying the people of God as well. There is a sifting of our profession of faith (see Matt. 7:21–23, 13:47–49) and a purging of our works (1 Cor. 3:13–15). Appropriately, therefore, verses 15,16 echo the 'entrance liturgies' of Psalms 15 and 24 in demanding comprehensive purity of life and conduct, especially in those areas that are the characteristic concerns of Isaiah (compare 1:16,17, 23).

Verses 17–24 in their immediate context describe the joyful relief in the aftermath of the broken siege. The king will reign over his whole land, no longer cooped up in Jerusalem (17). The foreign armies will be just a memory (18,19). Pilgrimages and festivals will be resumed in peace (20). But we are led to see more in these verses, both by the language of verses 21,22 and, especially, of verse 24 with its combination of God's enrichment, healing and forgiveness; and also because we know that in spite of verse 20 (which became a presumptuous belief in the inviolability of Jerusalem, compare Jer. 7:1–15) Jerusalem *was* historically destroyed in 587 BC by Babylon (and again in 70 AD by Rome). So again, it is to the *eternal* city of God that our 'eyes' are directed, where the 'King in his beauty' will be the Messiah himself (17). But the eyes that will see him will be those that are shut to evil (15). 'Blessed are the *pure* in heart, for *they* shall see God' (Matt. 5:8). By contrast, the wicked are aimless and without motive or means to keep them off the rocks (23).

THOUGHT: The confidence that God will save us comes only when he is acknowledged as Judge, Ruler and King (22).

34 The horror of judgement

Chapters 34 and 35 together form the climax to the prophetical oracles of this part of the book of Isaiah, before the historical interlude of chapters 36–39. Like the 'Apocalypse' of chapters 24–27, the climactic picture of salvation (chapter 35) is preceded by the grim reality of cosmic judgement (chapter 34). That the two are inseparably linked is shown by comparing 34:8 with 35:4.

Verses 1–4 begin with a summons reminiscent of 1:2 – a call to trial, which is universal not only in that it includes all mankind (2), but also all spiritual powers of evil (4). Though described as astral bodies ('hosts of heaven') their fall is as ignominious as falling, rotting leaves (compare also 24:21, 23, and the note on 27:1, and Matt. 24:29; Rev. 6:13, 14).

Verses 5–17: The judgement homes in upon Edom, whose relationships with Israel had been inveterately bitter. Notwithstanding the remembrance of fraternity (Deut. 23:7), there was hostility in Isaiah's time (2 Kings 16:6), and the way Edom took advantage of the Babylonian conquest of Jerusalem was neither forgotten nor forgiven (compare Ps. 137:7; Ezek. 25:12–14:35; Obad. 10–16). So this prophecy has its undoubted historical roots and, in the eventual destruction and desertion of Edom, its historical fulfilment. But Edom itself became symbolic of all that is anti-God and at enmity with his people (compare Heb. 12:16), and elements of this prophecy indicate that universal judgement is still in view. Verse 9, for example, evokes memories of the fate of Sodom and Gomorrah. The desolation of verses 11–15 recalls the predicted fate of Babylon (compare 13:19–22) – already the symbol of doomed human rebellion. Furthermore, the Hebrew words which are translated by 'confusion' and 'chaos' in verse 11 are the same words which are translated 'without form and void' in Genesis 1:2 (compare Jer. 4:23). Thus what is envisaged is a kind of retrogression, under God's wrath, to the unformed 'pre-creation' state of chaos. To add horror to such a thought, the prophet 'peoples' the scene with particularly unclean, repulsive and fearsome creatures (13–15).

If we find the imagery of this chapter repulsive, we need not doubt that so did its author, whose deliberate intention was to impress on us that the fate of the wicked who persist in rejection of God is unspeakably fearful. We may prefer to use other imagery, but the reality remains – as it did in the urgent preaching of Jesus himself.

THOUGHT: Ponder the effect such a chapter as this should have on the lethargy of our evangelism.

35 The joy of the redeemed

The darkness gives way to glory! The contrast between this chapter and the last is infinite, and yet they are necessarily parts of the same divine act. In both there is a transformation of nature: in chapter 34 it is plunged in destruction, moving backwards into chaos along with the judgement of the wicked (compare 2 Pet. 3:7–12); in chapter 35 it is renewed and virtually re-created for the benefit of the redeemed people of God (compare Rom. 8:21; 2 Pet. 3:13). In both cases it is the final act of God, vindication and restoration of his people from the midst of a hostile world – the ultimate 'Day of the Lord' (34:8; 35:4).

The original historical reference point of the prophecy, as of the great chapters from Isaiah 40 onwards, was the return of the Judean exiles from captivity in Babylon to Jerusalem. Since considerable distance and wilderness terrain lay between, the return was conceived as a new Exodus (compare 40:3–5; 41:17–20, etc.), only this time the desert would be carpeted with spring flowers, shaded with trees ('the glory of Lebanon', 1), abundant in water (6,7), and utterly safe (9). Clearly the language soars beyond the historical reality of the return from Exile, which became in time, along with the Exodus and other great acts of God in Israel's history, itself a pointer towards a reality which far transcended it – namely the final ingathering of all the Lord's redeemed to eternal, undisturbed joy (10).

Indeed, there is a mingling of the idea that the desert will be transformed for the benefit of the *redeemed*, with that of its being decked out for the coming of the *Lord* himself (2c, 4b). And when he comes, then more than nature will be transformed; miracles will restore the most crippling and intractable human deformities (5,6). No wonder there was amazement at precisely these miracles of Jesus (compare Mark 7:37)! And if John the Baptist were Elijah, then who, in view of Malachi 3:1; 4:5, could Jesus be? 'Behold, your God comes!' (compare Matt. 11:5). With the coming of Jesus, the messianic Kingdom of God is already inaugurated. The New Age has begun, but the end of the Old Age is yet to come. Meanwhile we live 'in the overlap', finding those 'waters in the desert' of God's provision, but looking forward to the 'everlasting joy' of entering Zion with the redeemed of the Lord.

THOUGHT: This symphony of joy and hope is also a call to perseverance. Ponder verse 3 in the context of its quotation in Hebrews 12:12.

36 Smooth words

The events of the Assyrian siege of Jerusalem in 701 BC which have lain behind so much of the oracles of the last few chapters are recounted here in a historical form which almost entirely derives from 2 Kings 18–20. 'The Rabshakeh' is a title, not a name, for a high official (2). On Eliakim and Shebna, the Judean royal officials, see 22:15–24.

The Rabshakeh's speech is a superb example of propaganda and subversion, and indicates a high degree of espionage – it even includes the words of Isaiah himself (10)! His points are as follows: (*a*) Words are no substitute for strategy and arms (5, – a taunt at Isaiah?). (*b*) Egypt is a useless ally (6) – something Isaiah had said repeatedly! (*c*) Hezekiah, supposedly trusting in the LORD (Yahweh), has destroyed his rural shrines (7)! This was a reference to Hezekiah's centralising reformation, which may well have been unpopular (compare 2 Chron. 29–31). (*d*) The difference in military strength is so great that Assyria can spare more horses than Judah can provide riders (9,10)! (*e*) How can they trust in Yahweh, when it is Yahweh himself who has sent the Assyrians – a very subtle and pointed use of Isaiah's words, albeit selective (10). Disregarding the officials, the Assyrian drives his message home to the listening citizens of Jerusalem (11–13), and continues: (*f*) Hezekiah is a fraud, not to be trusted (14,15). (*g*) The King of Assyria is really most benevolent! The imagery of verse 16 shows inside knowledge of characteristically Israelite aspirations (compare Mic. 4:4), though the promise of a land as good as their own (17) seriously underestimated the depth of Israel's attachment to the land promised to Abraham. (*h*) The final piercing question – can Yahweh conceivably be better than the gods of other people – including Samaria (wasn't that Yahweh anyway?)? Can they risk finding out (18–20)?

The instruction not to answer was wise, for the arguments are so subtle and such a twisted mixture of fact, half-truth, 'scripture' and enticement that the Israelites could not have begun to match them. The only answer would be found in the Lord's house (chapter 37).

THOUGHT: It sometimes happens that truths we have refused to hear from God himself are forced upon us by adversity (compare verse 6).

37:1–20 A model response

Despair drives the officials (even haughty Shebna) to the first sign of the repentance Isaiah had so much pleaded for (36:21,22), and Hezekiah joins them (1). The words of Hezekiah to Isaiah (3,4) are rich in meaning. They begin with a humble facing of facts (3). There is no presumption ('It may be that . . .'). There is an implied acceptance that only Isaiah has truly spoken the mind of God ('the Lord *your* God'). There is the continuing rock of faith in the one characteristic of their God, Yahweh, that sets him apart – he is the *living* God. Finally, there is an implied acceptance of Isaiah's prophecy of God's purging out a 'remnant', who now need his prayer. Isaiah's initial reply to this deputation of those who had so persistently refused his advice before is short, but graciously lacks any note of 'I told you so' (5–7). He confines himself to a simple prediction and exhortation to steady nerves. The oratory will flow later (22–29).

A temporary respite ensued when the Assyrian army withdrew to respond to an Egyptian intervention which failed. Sennacherib made sure, by a letter repeating the substance of the Rabshakeh's speech, that Hezekiah knew he would be back (8–13).

Hezekiah's response (14–20) is a model, both of what to do with 'circumstances beyond our control', and of prayer in such a situation. In the spirit of Psalm 55:22 he quite literally lays his problem out before God – his gesture both expressing and supporting his prayer (14, compare 17). His prayer begins and ends with concern for God's glory and his 'status' in the world – the mainspring of all intercessory prayer as well. Verse 16 is a deliberate recalling of snatches of Psalms and the language of worshipping faith. It already begins to reduce the problem to perspective. Verse 17 is almost requesting God to be as concerned for his own honour as he, Hezekiah, is! Verse 18 recounts the same facts about which the Rabshakeh had boasted, but sees an entirely different meaning in them – with the clarity of faith in the presence of the living God (19). After such a prelude, the main request (20) is lifted from the plane of selfishness or mere survival to an affirmation of the whole purpose of God in the history of Israel.

THOUGHT: Use Hezekiah's prayer as a pattern whenever you take a problem to the Lord. You will find it is then no longer your problem, but his.

37:21–38 The true perspective

Prayer such as Hezekiah's goes direct to the heart of God and in this case a reply was already on its way via Isaiah. The outburst of verses 22–29 is breathtaking in its poetic power and the 'insolence' of its content, given the human situation! Verse 22 either already envisages the ignominious retreat of Sennacherib after the blow of verse 36, or else refers to the temporary withdrawal that was the occasion of the letter. Either way it is a remarkable 'nose-thumbing' at the most powerful empire of the day! That done, the mocking questions of the Rabshakeh ('On whom do you rely?' 36:5) are returned with threatening force: 'Whom have you mocked? . . . the Holy One of Israel!' (23). The arrogance of Assyria is caught in what may have been a 'battle-song' – part of their propaganda machine (24,25). The song boasts of their 'many chariots', their engineering feats (25a) and extensive conquests. However, just as in 10:5–19, God not only claims to be in control of the present (28), but to have been working out his purpose from the distant past (26) which, for the Assyrians, will mean a very nasty future (29). This sovereignty over the whole span of time becomes a major theme of the later chapters of the book.

That should have been a sufficient answer to Hezekiah's prayer! But, either at the same time, or, more probably, later, two further prophecies are addressed to him. Verse 30 means that the invasion will cost only two harvests. There may be an implied comparison with the Sabbatical or Jubilee year, which required trust in God's ability to provide (compare Lev. 25:1–12). This is combined with a reiteration of Isaiah's familiar 'remnant' theology (31). Finally, the promise of complete deliverance is spelled out (33,34), and the reason for it specified clearly (35), 'lest any man should boast'.

The cause of the disaster which led to Sennacherib's sudden withdrawal is not related (some evidence suggests it may have been a plague), for, to the author, *who* caused it was more significant than *what* caused it. The assassination of verse 38 took place in 682 BC – some twenty years after the prophecy of verse 7.

THOUGHT: 'We despaired of life itself . . . But that was to make us rely not on ourselves but on God who raises the dead' (2 Cor. 1:8,9).

38 Healing for Hezekiah

Though there is some difficulty over the precise chronology, it is most probable that the events of chapters 38,39 should be regarded as having taken place *before* the siege of 701 BC. The reason for the inversion is that chapters 36,37 refer to the events that form the background to the immediately preceding oracles, while chapter 39 predicts the rise of Babylon and hints at the Exile, which forms the background to chapter 40. Chapters 36–39 are thus the 'hinge' of the book.

Hezekiah's illness has something of the story of Job about it (though Hezekiah had a more competent comforter in Isaiah – theologically and medically!) His prayer in verse 3 is a plea based on his own record (compare Job 31), which the facts bore out. But in his later psalm of thanksgiving (10–20), there is the suggestion that his distress was caused by unforgiven sin (17b, and compare verses 13,14 with Ps. 32:3), as well as the imminence of death. Like Job, he reaches the point of despair in the awareness that the God with whom he pleads is the God who has caused the situation (15a).

The answer to his prayer took several forms, which are perhaps chronologically confused (verses 21,22 should possibly be read before verse 7). There was Isaiah's prophetic word, promising prolonged life as well as national deliverance (5,6), accompanied both by a simple medical act (21) and a miraculous sign (8). We are given no further information about either – that is, whether the poultice was the 'effective cause' of his recovery, or simply 'sacramental' of the Lord's healing (as, for example, the use of oil in Jas. 5:14), and what were the mechanics of the 'sign' of the shadow on the steps. Interestingly, in the light of James 5:15,16 Hezekiah's recovery included forgiveness as well as healing (17).

Hezekiah's recoil from death and the grave ('Sheol') is understandable in view of the general Old Testament view of them as the total negation of all that is good in this life. An insight such as 26:19 had hardly penetrated yet, let alone the later Christian revelation of resurrection.

Notes: Verses 15b and 16a are full of difficulties; compare the different translations. Verse 20 shows that the Psalm was intended for corporate use.

THOUGHT: 'I am the Lord your healer' (Exod. 15:26)
'I am the resurrection and the life' (John 11:25)

39 Caught off guard

Babylon at this time (that is, 705–702 BC) was as yet only a vassal part of the Assyrian Empire, but this king Merodach-baladan is known to have tried to instigate revolt against Assyria. The embassy to Hezekiah was part of that strategy, and it was in fact Hezekiah's joining in the revolt which led to the attempted reprisals by Sennacherib in 701.

The act of Hezekiah (2) may have indicated his willingness to throw his resources behind the revolt. Or it may have stemmed from a childish exhibitionism that responded to flattery. Even the staunchest heroes among the Lord's people have their exploitable weak spots (compare Gideon, Judg. 8:24–27). 2 Chronicles 32:31 certainly interprets the event as a 'testing' of his heart.

At any rate, it brought the disapproval of God through Isaiah, to whom it was yet another example of the ineradicable habit of placing human security before divine promises – quite apart from the political folly of so complete an exposure of the resources and treasures of the state (4). Thus Isaiah is given his long–range prophecy of the rape of Jerusalem by the very Babylonians whom Hezekiah was trying to impress – an event still over a century distant, but whose shadow must have been a sad burden to Isaiah. The cynicism of Hezekiah's reply is hard to credit to the man of chapter 37. Such is the honesty of Scripture. It does not 'gild' even the few kings regarded as otherwise good and godly. Perhaps his reply may be regarded as embarrassed bravado at having his regal showing-off transformed into a prophetic symbol of future doom.

For us the lesson is perhaps to be aware that though our faith, like Hezekiah's, may withstand frontal attacks and obvious enemies, we may be disarmed and destroyed by a touch of flattery (compare the note on Prov. 27).

THOUGHT: 'What have you that you did not receive? If then you received it, why do you boast as if it were not a gift?' (1 Cor. 4:7).

Questions for further study and discussion on Isaiah 32–39

1. Is there motivation in 32:15–17 for those who are filled with the Spirit of the Messiah to work for social righteousness and peace?

2. See note on 33:11. What forms of social evil are particularly self-destructive? Should this form part of the content of our moral polemic against them?

3. Do you find it difficult to regard both chapters 34 and 35 as part of the acts of the same God? If so, consider the cross and resurrection from the same perspective.

4. How do you react to the pictures of judgement contained in chapter 34 and other places? What can you detect of Isaiah's emotions as he proclaimed these messages? Should the church proclaim a message of judgement – and if so, how?

5. Which arguments most tempt you to stop trusting God (compare ch. 36)? How do you counter them? What did Jesus do in similar situations?

6. Compare Hezekiah's prayer (37:14–20) with those of Abraham (Gen. 18:23–31), Moses (Exod. 32:11–14, 33:12–16), Jehoshaphat (2 Chron. 20:5–12), Jeremiah (Jer. 32:17–25), Daniel (Dan. 9:4–19) and the early church (Acts 4:23–31). What do you learn from this?

7. Which features of Hezekiah's sickness, prayer and psalm remain valid for us, and which are transformed by New Testament revelation?

8. What have you found most challenging and encouraging in your study of these chapters of Isaiah?